The aim of *Buddhist Perception of Nature* is to reach as many people as possible, so please feel free to use any material in this book, with appropriate attribution. We would appreciate a copy for our records.

Published by Buddhist Perception of Nature

Edited by Shann Davies

Production by Earl & Associates

Designed by Buddhist Perception of Nature with Earl & Associates

ISBN 962-7257-02-8

The publisher wishes to thank Sir Peter Scott, Miss Fleur Cowles, Khun Sirijit Waramonti, Khun Mongol Wongkalasin, Mr Adrian Dyson and Ollie Dwiggins for permission to use their works of art as illustrations, also Mr Tony Martorano for his photography and Mr Brian Livingston-Wilcox for the book's design.

Cover: Buddhist Perception of Nature by Ollie Dwiggins

Acknowledgements

Buddhist Perception of Nature project personnel are grateful to Mr. and Mrs. Hans Michael Jebsen for their support of the project's objectives, and for making this publication possible.

We also express here our gratitude to the following institutions, organisations and individuals for their support of our work:

INSTITUTIONS

Beldon Fund
Buddhists Concerned for Animals
C S Fund
Council for Religious and Cultural Affairs of His Holiness The Dalai Lama
Friends Of The Earth (Hong Kong)
Information Office of His Holiness The Dalai Lama
International Consultancy on Religion, Education and Culture
International Institute for Environment and Development (IIED)
International Network for Religion and Animals (INRA)
Munro Foundation
Offices of Tibet in London, New Delhi, New York, Tokyo and Zurich
Sacharuna Foundation
Wildlife Conservation International, Division of New York Zoological Society (NYZS)
Wildlife Fund Thailand (WFT)
World Wildlife Fund
World Wide Fund for Nature Hong Kong
WWF India
United Nations Environment Programme (UNEP)

ORGANISATIONS

Earl & Associates
Graphic Communication Limited
Hilton International Co.
Hongkong Hilton
Hyatt Regency New Delhi
IBM Thailand
Kodak (Far East) Ltd.
The Mayfair Regent Hotel, New York
Minor Holdings Group (Thailand)
Presko Public Relations
Regent International Hotels
The Regent of Bangkok
Schroders Asia Ltd.
Thai Airways International

INDIVIDUALS

Dr. Solly Angel
Dr. Gerald O. Barney
Mr. Gus Buder
Mr. and Mrs. Robert Burns
Dr. Tyrone McNally Cashman
Mr. Peter Carre
Miss Fleur Cowles
Mr. Richard J. Croft, Jr.
Miss Shann Davies
Mr. John Dolfin
Ms. Ollie Dwiggins
Mr. Adrian Dyson
Prof. J. Ronald Engel
Mr. William Heering
Dr. Nay Htun
Ms. Elizabeth Jones
Ms. Sandy Kidner
Mr. L. Lee
Dr. Boonsong Lekagul
Mr. John Loudon
Mr. Dario Mariotto
Mr. Tony Martorano
Miss Yvette Mimieux
Mr. Kenneth S. Moss
J. M.
Mr. Clyde Min
Ms. Selma Olson
Mr. Martin Palmer
Mr. Harry Rolnick
R. R.
Sir Peter and Lady Scott
Dr. George B. Schaller
Ms. Linda Siddall
Mr. Henry Steiner
Mr. Larry Tchou
Khun Mechai Viravaidya
Mr. Michael Van Walt Van Praag
Ms. Victoria Wakefield
Ms. Martha Walsh
Mr. Wu Tai Chow

Contents

The Rolex Awards for Enterprise

A winner in the category of The Environment
Nancy Nash
for *Buddhist Perception of Nature*
Geneva 1987

INTRODUCTION

by Sir Peter Scott

THIS BOOK and the project which brought it about — the *Buddhist Perception of Nature* — are important new educational approaches to the ecological disasters resulting from man's destruction of nature, and what can and must be done to conserve the world's living resources.

It may seem surprising that a new educational perspective employs teachings and traditions, some of which date back more than 2,500 years. As an international movement of significance, conservation of nature, spearheaded by governments and private groups, is at most a few decades old, and is still in the process of being generally accepted. So why, in this most modern of causes, with immediate problems to be solved, should we apply our thoughts to ancient teachings?

The simple answer is that although conservation efforts increase they are outmatched by the continuing destruction of the environment. Our current attempts to solve the problem are not enough to do the job.

Conservation work, for the most part, has been mounted in response to crisis, focusing on biological problems and proposing technological solutions with varying degrees of success. Yet the unsolved and ongoing, even accelerating, destruction of nature and natural resources has clearly not yet been tackled effectively on a global scale.

One reason for this is conservation's newness on the scene — although many of us now know how tragically late it has come for so many animal and plant species and their habitats. Another reason is the movement's limited manpower and resources. Most of the world's human population have yet to realise that conservation is an essential element of human progress — in economics, development, sustainable yields of food, in short the very life-support systems of our planet.

The message is valid, and vital for the well being of people now and for future generations, but it is widely ignored. Often its emphasis overlooks the various cultural, social and perceptual factors in the problem and in the potential solutions.

Enlightened government and business leaders may be persuaded to become active in protection of nature because of the work's importance for future economic, or scientific purposes, but it is unlikely they will act solely for those reasons. People who protect, or destroy, do so for many different reasons. As His Holiness the Dalai Lama reminds us in his Declaration, plain human greed is a major cause of destruction of the natural world. This and lack of respect for other people and other living forms is often the result of an impoverished cultural environment.

Among those who actively protect, we find conservationists who never go near the wilderness, but feel a responsibility to help save it for those who do. We find pragmatic business people who want to protect their investments. Children around the world often bluntly, charmingly state that they want to protect animals because they love them.

There are scientists, leaders in their fields, who support conservation for one reason: to maintain the world's genetic diversity. I know wildlife biologists and other scientists, among them the most gifted professionals at work, who were drawn to conservation because of its aesthetic appeal.

Many deep philosophical elements are involved, and education stands out as the most important long-term ingredient if life on earth is to continue.

The *Buddhist Perception of Nature* and its products such as this volume, are of great importance to the world conservation community, not only for Buddhist areas, but for wherever the health of our planet is threatened.

Here we have conservation education in all senses of the phrase, beginning in the home, and reaching out into formal instruction and leadership levels. Conservation is set in a cultural matrix, with emphasis on accepted traditions and codes of conduct.

The impressive scholarship in the contributions from Dr. Chatsumarn Kabilsingh, in her summary of the Buddhist role in protection of the natural world, and of Dr. Nay Htun, in his outline of the present state of the environment, serve to underscore the book's message: Conservation as a way of life increases the quality of life, and the Buddhist precepts of harmony and care are being increasingly reflected in modern environmental management policies.

It has been my pleasure to follow the *Buddhist Perception of Nature* project since its beginning, before it had a title. In 1979 the project originator, Nancy Nash, working as a consultant for the World Wildlife Fund proposed that conservation should enlist the help of the world's religions. She also proposed that WWF should make contact with China, and then personally established the contact. It kept her busy for a number of years and earned her the title "Miss Panda". Next Nancy was asked to help set up WWF's organisation in Hong Kong.

Her 'religion-to-help-conservation' project had to wait until 1985, when it was formally inaugurated. Within two years this project has helped to formulate some of the most important Buddhist teachings regarding man's responsibilities to nature, and has increased public awareness of environmental ethics wherever it has become known.

The ethical basis of conservation has always been of fundamental importance to me in my life and work, so it is very gratifying to see this so strongly represented in the project's goals and in this book.

His Holiness The Dalai Lama, Buddhist but much more — an internationally respected spiritual leader — has provided inspiration, encouragement and support for the work throughout the project's development, and we can only hope that other religious leaders will follow the example of his Declaration on environmental ethics published in this book, so appropriately called *Tree of Life*.

Sir Peter Scott
Slimbridge, England

Sir Peter Scott, CBE, DSC, *is a pioneer of international conservation. He has been involved within the International Union for Conservation of Nature (IUCN) for more than 30 years and was one of the founders of the World Wildlife Fund (WWF) 20 years ago. He is a professional painter, author, broadcaster and lecturer. He was trained in biology and art. He is now in his 78th year.*

An Ethical Approach to Environmental Protection

by His Holiness The Dalai Lama

Peace and survival of life on earth as we know it are threatened by human activities which lack a commitment to humanitarian values.

Destruction of nature and natural resources results from ignorance, greed and lack of respect for the earth's living things.

This lack of respect extends even to earth's human descendants, the future generations who will inherit a vastly degraded planet if world peace does not become a reality, and destruction of the natural environment continues at the present rate.

Our ancestors viewed the earth as rich and bountiful, which it is. Many people in the past also saw nature as inexhaustibly sustainable, which we now know is the case only if we care for it.

It is not difficult to forgive destruction in the past which resulted from ignorance. Today however, we have access to more information, and it is essential that we re-examine ethically what we have inherited, what we are responsible for, and what we will pass on to coming generations.

Clearly this is a pivotal generation. Global communication is possible, yet confrontations more often than meaningful dialogues for peace take place.

Our marvels of science and technology are matched if not outweighed by many current tragedies, including human starvation in some parts of the world, and extinction of other life forms.

Exploration of outer space takes place at the same time as the earth's own oceans, seas, and fresh water areas grow increasingly polluted, and their life forms are still largely unknown or misunderstood.

Many of the earth's habitats, animals, plants, insects, and even micro-organisms that we know as rare may not be known at all by future generations. We have the capability, and the responsibility. We must act before it is too late.

This message, from His Holiness Tenzin Gyatso, Fourteenth Dalai Lama of Tibet, is dated 5 June 1986, in recognition of World Environment Day, and that day's 1986 theme, Peace and The Environment.

How Buddhism Can Help Protect Nature

By Dr. Chatsumarn Kabilsingh

WAT PHAI LOM is a Buddhist temple not far from Bangkok which welcomes thousands of visitors from afar every year. The visitors are birds, open-billed storks. When residing at Wat Phai Lom during autumn and winter months, their droppings white-wash trees and temple buildings.

The monks do not mind, and bird-lovers celebrate the sight. Open-billed storks would be extinct in Thailand but for the fact their last remaining breeding ground is within the sanctuary of this temple.

Ecologists point out it is scientifically important to save this species of bird, whose sole diet is a local, rice-devouring species of snail. Without the storks, the snails would proliferate, then pesticides would be brought in, and an unnecessary, poisonous cycle would go into effect.

Buddhist precepts of personal and social conduct can take much of the credit for saving the open-billed stork in Thailand, a country which has suffered tremendous destruction of the natural environment in recent decades.

Forests, for example, covered 80 percent of the land 50 years ago; today forestland has been reduced to just over 20 percent. Many bird, animal, and plant species are in danger of extinction, and some have already disappeared.

The most tragic consequences of degraded and disappearing nature and natural resources are seen in various human rural communities where survival is a struggle.

Changing ecological conditions have resulted in frequent flooding in Bangkok; it's an inconvenience. But in parts of the country's northeast, a degraded natural environment means that annual rains do not arrive on schedule, crops fail, and many people experience a borderline existence.

While so much has been destroyed, it is worth observing that even more could have been lost, and more quickly, given the modern world's eagerness for exploitation and little regard for the consequences.

It is likely that, like the open-billed stork, much of what still survives of the natural world here is linked, in varying degrees, to the influence of Buddhism, the philosophy's focus on awareness, attitudes, and actions which should never harm, and ideally should actively help all life on earth.

This is not to say that careless, even greedy individuals involved in destruction do not consider themselves Buddhists. Just as codes of conduct regarding protection of nature vary from religion to religion, interpretations of those codes vary from person to person.

In all belief systems, human nature is diverse. In Buddhism, among the world's estimated ½ billion faithful, individuals range from the highly enlightened and pious to those who don't know what else to call themselves — a group which can be described as "Buddhists by birth certificate".

Buddhism also encourages individual perceptions, even questions and challenges on the part of each practitioner, because enlightenment is a personal path. Comparative religious studies find this an unusual feature in a major religion which also has established instutional structures.

Embodied in Buddhism, however, is much ecologists and other conservation experts explain is urgently needed if destruction of the natural environment is to be halted, and life on earth as we know it is to continue.

Teachings emphasise the importance of coexisting with nature, rather than conquering it. Devout Buddhists admire a conserving lifestyle, rather than one which is profligate.

The very core of Buddhism evolves around compassion, encouraging a better respect for and tolerance of every human being and living thing sharing the planet.

Wherever Buddhism is influential, studies will usually show some direct benefit for the natural world. In Sri Lanka, predominantly Buddhist, crowded by western standards, wildlife has not been virtually eliminated, as it has been in many parts of the world. The reason, according to researchers, is the country's largely religious and devout population.

Formal protection generally results from government action, but such actions, it is felt, would never have made much effect if they were not readily accepted by the people. Successful conservation there is based on deep philosophical convictions.[1]

Many of our *Buddhist Perception of Nature* project's Tibetan research colleagues can point to the time, in living memory, when herds of wild blue sheep, yak, deer and flocks of migrating birds would travel with Tibetan nomads, or land in the midst of human settlements — apparently sensing they were safe. For the most part they were safe from harm, because the country was Buddhist.

The situation since the Chinese takeover has tragically changed, and Tibet is now described as "ecologically devastated" in many respects. In a special report for the U N Commission on Human Rights, it is noted that large areas are now deforested, and "a once flourishing wildlife seems to have been virtually wiped out..."[2]

Buddhism's benefits to nature protection throughout the faith's history might be described as effective, in a largely passive role. Recently and increasingly, however, influential Buddhists are speaking out on the subject and helping bring about recognition of the active, even dynamic role the philosophy could play in conservation.

"Today more than ever before," His Holiness The Dalai Lama told a reporter, "life must be characterised by a sense of Universal Responsibility, not only nation to nation and human to human, but also human to other forms of life."(3)

Social critic and author Sulak Sivaraksa, described as "a Thai Buddhist voice on Asia and a World of Change", believes that however complex the world has become, the message of Buddhism is relevant, indeed even more relevant than earlier, and an important catalyst of social unity and progress.(4)

Concerned about destruction of the natural environment, and convinced Buddhism, in an active role, can bring about improved protection, Khun Sulak has added to his writings on the subject a special slide show and taped message illustrating proper Buddhist awareness, attitudes, and actions concerning Nature.

"Whether they are conscious of it or not," the narrative goes, "there is a kind of Buddhist revolt against the deterioration of Nature. It is a small revolt, because it has not yet affected the overall statistics."

"But still, this peaceful commitment means something, and if it is taken seriously, it can help bring about a strong conservationist movement in our country."

His Excellency Yasuhiro Nakasone, Prime Minister of Japan, included in his address at the Commemorative Anniversary of the United Nations in 1985, an eloquent and moving call for all nations, religions, and peoples to join together to ensure that the beauty and diversity of earth will continue.

Again we find Buddhism brought into the message, one which also urges "a new global ethic" so that the Twentieth Century may be known "as the era when coexistence and mutual respect were achieved among all peoples for the first time, and when men found a proper balance with Nature."(5)

Ancient as Buddhist lessons are, their value in modern life and contemporary needs is increasingly recognised. One reason for this, according to Thai scholar Piyadassi, is that "The Buddha emphasises the practical aspect of His teaching, the application of knowledge to life, looking into life and not merely at it."(6)

British author H. G. Wells found the subject worthy of study, and summarised, "The fundamental teaching of Gauthama (The Buddha)...is clear and in closest harmony with modern ideas. It is beyond dispute the achievement of one of the most penetrating intelligences the world has ever known."(7)

Buddhism, moreover, brings a special dimension to any studies or projects such as the *Buddhist Perception of Nature*, involving education. It is the duty of every practising Buddhist to seek to replace ignorance with knowledge and wisdom. Teachers are respected; in the case of the faith's greatest teachers, revered.

To provide teachers with the tools they need to lead their students to conservation practises, project scholars have the task of thoroughly researching the vast and rich Buddhist literature, involving several languages, and early texts reaching back in some cases more than 2,500 years.

Research is the first stage, followed by assembly of the materials. For the first time, Buddhist teachings about humankind's needs and responsibilities concerning animals and plants, forests and water resources, indeed the whole natural environment, are being compiled by the *Buddhist Perception of Nature* project to produce comprehensive, educational instruments.

The wealth of material scholars are discovering is not surprising when one considers Buddhism's focus on compassion, the forest-dwelling and meditation in natural surroundings important to many in the *Sangha* — the order of monks — and the rich symbolism associated with many species of animals and plants.

Monks, for example, are forbidden to cut down trees, and know well the story of a monk long ago, who cut a tree's main branch. The spirit of the tree complained to Buddha, that by doing so, the monk had cut off his child's arm.(8)

Another teaching relates that travellers, after having rested in the shade of a large banyan, on leaving began to cut down the tree. Their actions were condemned. The tree had given them shade, much like a friend, and to harm a friend is indeed an act of evil.(9)

Anguttara Nikaya provides a similar episode:

> *"Long ago, Brahman Dhamika, Rajah Koranya, had a king banyan called Steadfast, and the shade of its widespread branches was cool and lovely.*
>
> *Its shelter broadened to twelve leagues. None guarded its fruit, and none hurt another for its fruit.*
>
> *Now then came a man who ate his fill of fruit, broke down a branch, and went his way.*
>
> *Thought the spirit dwelling in that tree: How amazing, how astonishing it is, that a man should be so evil as to break off a branch of the tree, after eating his fill. Suppose the tree were to bear no more fruit.*
>
> *And the tree bore no more fruit."*(10)

Such teachings remind Buddhists — monks and lay people alike — of the importance of showing respect for trees which provide food, shade and protection not only for people, but for all forest-dwellers.

The results of lack of respect for trees are clearly evident today. When large areas of forest are destroyed, erosion often follows, degrading watersheds, and ultimately making farming fruitless. Animal and plant species, losing their habitats, often disappear.

Although Buddhism took root in the soil of humanity more than 2,500 years ago, at a time when people generally lived closer to nature than many do today, the consequences of improper attitudes and actions regarding the earth were known, and described in the story of a Brahmin who asked The Buddha about the cause of human decrease. This is how The Buddha answered:

> *"Since folk are ablaze with unlawful lusts, overwhelmed by depraved longings, depressed by wrong doctrines, on such as these the*

sky rains down not steadily. It is hard to get a meal. The crops are bad, afflicted with mildew and grown to mere stubs. Accordingly, many come to their end."(11)

Ideally, because of the important precept that it is wrong to take life, or even cause to take life, devout Buddhists try to live on a diet of fruit, vegetables and grains. Even in this strict observance however, awareness, mindfulness, comes in.

In consuming fruits and grains, strict practitioners should be careful not to destroy the growth of such foods. Fruit from which seed has been removed, for example, is allowable.(12)

The Buddhist rules regarding consumption of foods are lengthy and complicated, and are being examined in project activities. The most important point to remember in an introduction, such as this text, is that all human activity should be with a sense of respect and reverence for all life, with a feeling of conservation and not exploitation.

For Buddhism, all animals are within the field of human perception, with an opportunity someday to gain enlightenment. Higher beings though humans may be, Buddhism teaches that man is a part of entire nature, disregarding or abusing natural laws or trying to conquer nature at his own peril.

Buddhist Perception of Nature's chief Tibetan scholar, Ven. Karma Gelek Yuthok, provides to the subject some lovely, even tender, stanzas from the *Mahayana* traditions about compassion for living things:

> *"Since the doctrine of Buddha specifies compassion, those who take refuge in it should forsake harming the sentient beings with a compassionate heart."*(13)

Further explaining the importance of abandoning harm to living things, Tsongkhapa(14) taught:

> *"The abandonment of harm to sentient beings is, to foresake all thoughts and deeds as — beating men or beasts, binding with ropes, trapping and imprisonment, piercing the noses, overburdening with loads beyond their strength, and similar activities."*(15)

Similarly, Dzogchen Patul Jigme Wangpo, in his text called *The Oral Transmission of Samandrabhadra*, relates:

> *"As it has been said that having taken refuge in The Doctrine, one should abandon harm to the living beings, the acts that are harmful to the other beings should not be done even in ones dreams... persevere with strong efforts to protect oneself from such acts."*

Not doing harm is a stage reaching to higher Buddhist attitudes towards all living things — loving kindness, compassion and altruism. On the attitude of loving kindness, The Buddha has said:

> *"Making, all the time, a rich and extensive offering with all that can be found in the billions of worlds to the supreme noble beings,*

this merit cannot match one moment of loving kindness."(16)

Another well known and much loved teaching which exemplifies the central core of compassion in Buddhism is:

> *"Thus, as a mother with her own life guards the life of her own child, let all embracing thoughts for all that lives be thine."*(17)

Two and a half millennia ago The Buddha taught disciples that the material world — earth and universe — included the worlds of "formations", "beings", and "space". That much in such ancient teachings is apparently found by many modern physicists to be compatible with the newest advances in their field of study, is less important to Buddhists than the continuing, even growing, need for human attitudes of loving kindness in our modern world.

Centuries before contamination of the earth's water would be the widespread threat to health and life that it is today, The Buddha set down rules forbidding pollution of water resources.(18) Even detailed descriptions of how a toilet should be built were provided, specifically to protect a healthy environment.(19)

Buddhism flourished early in settings of abundant Nature, and many teachings use examples and similes from Nature to convey important messages:

> *"Suppose a pool of water, turbid, stirred up and muddied, exists. Just so a turbid mind is. Suppose a pool of water, pure, tranquil and unstirred, where a man sees oysters and shells, pebbles and gravels, and schools of fish. Just so is an untroubled mind."*(20)

As for human souls in stages of growth and enlightenment, the lotus, sacred to both Hindus and Buddhists, is the symbol:

> *"...in a pond of blue lotus, or in a pond of red and white lotus, a few blue, red, or white lotus are born in water, grown in water, altogether immersed. A few blue, red and white lotus are born in water, grow there, and reach the surface — standing up, rising, undefiled."*(21)

Many of the earth's most famous animals appear in The Buddha's teachings — tiger, elephant, and lion for example. Compassion and loving kindness are expressed for all, and in a certain place The Buddha was said to have compared his own behaviour with that of a lion's —

> *"He roars with the idea, let me not cause the destruction of tiny creatures wandering astray"*

— and even claimed the word "lion" was a term for The Buddha.(22)

Among the beautiful expressions in Buddhist literature showing mutual relation and interdependence of humankind and wildlife, there was early on a realisation that survival of certain species was in danger, and that losing such creatures diminishes the earth.

Scholars with the Pali Text Society, London, provide this particularly lovely translation of a stanza from the *Khuddakapàtha*:

Tree of Life, by Miss Fleur Cowles, an artist known and appreciated internationally. The original of this painting is now in a private collection, and the Buddhist Perception Of Nature personnel are grateful it may be reproduced here.

"Come back, O Tigers!, to the woods again, and let it not be leveled with the plain. For without you, the axe will lay it low. You, without it, forever homeless go."

Buddhism has always celebrated the richness and diversity of the earth, and the lotus is only one among the many plant species of great symbolic importance.

All Buddhist literature records that The Buddha was born in the forest, in a grove of Sal, lovely straight backed trees with large leaves. According to legend, as soon as he was born he could walk, and in the wake of his first seven steps lotuses sprang up. Meditation as a youth was in the shade of the "Jambo", one of the myrtle of which there are around 650 species.

The Buddha's further study was in the company of the Banyan, and enlightenment and Buddhahood were achieved under the spreading branches of a tree recognised for its special, symbolic place in human faith even in its scientific name, (*Ficus religiousa*). Also known as the Bo, Boddhi or Peepul, this tree is sacred in both Buddhism and Hinduism.

With all of these species we find an example of the faith's role in protection. Because of the important symbolic value they have in the life of Buddha, they are respected, and no devout follower would deliberately harm them.

It has been interesting to learn in our researches that there seems to be a twofold way of expressing and describing nature and the natural environment in the texts — a straightforward description, and then in many cases, an analogy.

Both are drawn from what was known of life and natural surroundings of the time, and largely in the northern areas of Jambudipa, or India, and yet demonstrate an extraordinary intellectual grasp of the interdependence of life altogether, at all times.

Early Buddhists were also, clearly, deeply appreciative of Nature's beauty and diversity. In the *Sutta-Nipata*, one of the earliest texts known, The Buddha says:

"Know ye the grasses and the trees...Then know ye the worms, and the moths, and the different sort of ants...Know ye also the four-footed animals small and great...the serpents...the fish which range in the water...the birds that are borne along on wings and move through the air....."

We have abbreviated above a long passage in which, for each kind of creature, The Buddha taught,

"(Know ye) the marks that constitute species are theirs, and their species are manifold..."(23)

The *Jakata*, the richly narrated Birth Stories of Buddhism, have inspired some of the world's most beautiful art, and are abundant with poetic appreciations of the beauty of Nature. In the edition edited by Professor E. B. Cowell for the Pali Text Society in 1957, passage after passage of volumes IV and V celebrate forests and waters, and the earth's wild creatures.

Here we find an area of the earth called "Garden of Delight", where grass is ever green, in forests grow all trees whose fruit is good to eat, the streams are sweet and clean — "blue as beryl" — with shoals of disporting fish. Nearby is:

> *"...a region overrun and beautified with all manner of trees and flowering shrubs and creepers, resounding with the cries of swans, ducks and geese..."*

Next is reported the fame of an area, "yielding from its soil all manner of herbs, overspread with many a tangle of flowers," and listing a rich variety of wild animals — antelope and elephant, gaur, buffalo, deer, yak, lion, and rhinoceros, then tiger, panther, bear, hyena, otter, hare and more.

If such scenes seem "other worldly" it is because, through ignorance, greed, and lack of respect for the earth, the world's growing human population has already transformed many of the earth's gardens of delight into poisoned fields, sterile, incapable of sustaining Nature's rich diversity.

That so much of the earth has already been destroyed, and destruction is actually increasing, is insupportable for Buddhists or people of any persuasion or belief who seek knowledge and wisdom, and who feel a sense of responsibility for the condition of life on this planet now and for future generations.

In *Buddhist Perception of Nature* research we are discovering and compiling teachings which in many ways also provide shocking reminders of how much we have lost of the natural world, and in such a brief space of time. This is one of the many lessons being learned, and it adds to a feeling of urgency to complete our research, and place good educational materials into the hands of teachers who will use them well.

By doing our part to bring to light the ancient Buddhist teachings which are as valid today as they have always been, in widening circles Buddhism can be an active element in proper conservation of the natural environment.

By sharing the fruits of our work with others, we look forward to a world acceptance of an environmental ethic that will replace ignorance with knowledge, greed with generosity, and lack of respect for the earth with attitudes of compassion and loving kindness — for all life.

Dr. Chatsumarn Kabilsingh, chief Thai scholar for the Buddhist Perception of Nature Project, teaches Religion and Philosophy as a member of the Faculty of Liberal Arts, at Thammasat University, Bangkok. She is also the author of a number of popular and scholarly articles on Buddhism, the translator of the Lotus Sutra, and the Tao Te-Ching into Thai, and the author of the book, Study of Buddhist Nuns: Monastic Rules.

Footnotes:

1. Moyle, P and Senanayke, F R in FAO's TIGERPAPER, October 1980
2. TIBET: THE FACTS, by the Scientific Buddhist Association (London) 1984
3. FAR EASTERN ECONOMIC REVIEW, 3 August 1979, p. 23
4. Sulak Sivaraksa, SIAMESE RESURGENCE, published by the Asian Cultural Forum on Development (Bangkok) 1985
5. See page 16
6. Piyadassi, BUDDHISM A LIVING MESSAGE (Bangkok)
7. Nigosian, S A, WORLD RELIGIONS, published by Edward Arnold (London) 1975

8. Pacittiya, Bhutagama Vagga, THAI TRIPITAKA, Vol 2, page 347
9. *Ibid*, Vol 27, p 370
10. Anguttara Nikaya, GRADUAL SAYINGS, Vol 3, p 262
11. *Ibid*, Vol 1, p 142
12. THAI TRIPITAKA, VII, p 8
13. Tsongkhapa, GREAT EXPOSITIONS ON THE GRADUAL PATH
14. The great teacher and revitalizer of Buddhism in Tibet, 14th century A D
15. *Ibid*
16. SAMADHIRAJA SUTRA, Vol 11, Dege Version
17. KHUNDDAKAPATHA (London) by the Pali Text Society, 1960
18. GRADUAL SAYINGS, Vol 26:104, p 174
19. *Ibid*, Vol 7, p 48 *Vinaya Pataka*
20. *Op. cit.*, Vol 1, pp 6-7
21. Nissagiya 15, SACRED BOOKS OF THE BUDDHISTS (SBB), Mahavagga, XIV, p 9
22. Woodward, F L (Tr) *Ibid*, Vol V, pp 23-24
23. Fausboll, V (tr), published by Motilal Banarsidass (Delhi) 1968.

From the Address by Japanese Prime Minister, H.E. Yasuhiro Nakasone, at the Commemorative Session of the 40th Anniversary of the United Nations, 23 October 1985:

"Our generation is recklessly destroying the natural environment which has evolved over the course of millions of years and is essential for our survival.

Our soil, water, air, flora and fauna are being subjected to the most barbaric attack since the earth was created. This folly can only be called suicidal.

If we are to preserve our irreplacable Earth and ensure the survival of mankind, I believe we must create a new global ethic and devise systems to support it.

Let us act today so that future historians can look back on the closing years of the Twentieth Century as the era when co-existence and mutual respect were achieved among all peoples for the first time and when men found a proper balance with nature.

We Japanese derive our beliefs and philosophy from traditions handed down by our ancestors over thousands of years, and from later influences of Confucianism and Buddhism. Basic to our philosophy is the concept that man is born by grace of the great universe.

We Japanese generally believe that the great natural universe is our home, and that all living things should co-exist in harmony with the natural universe. We believe that all living things — humans, animals, trees, grasses — are essentially brothers and sisters.

I doubt that this philosophy is unique to the Japanese. I believe that better understanding of it could contribute much to the creation of universal values for our international community.

The human potential for creativity is distributed evenly among all peoples in all lands, and all the different religious beliefs and artistic traditions in the world are equally unique and equally valuable.

The starting point for world peace is, I believe, a recognition of this diversity of human culture and a humble attitude of mutual appreciation and respect.

Are we not destroying our environment on an unprecedented scale, and perhaps endangering the survival of all life on this planet? As a political leader, I cannot but feel a deep sense of responsibility for the situation I am witnessing.

Thus I ask you to join me in a vow. Let us vow to work together so that, in the middle of the next century, when Halley's Comet completes another orbit and once again sweeps by our planet, our children and grandchildren will be able to look up at it and report that the Earth is one, and that mankind everywhere is co-existing in harmony and working for the well-being of all life on this verdant globe."

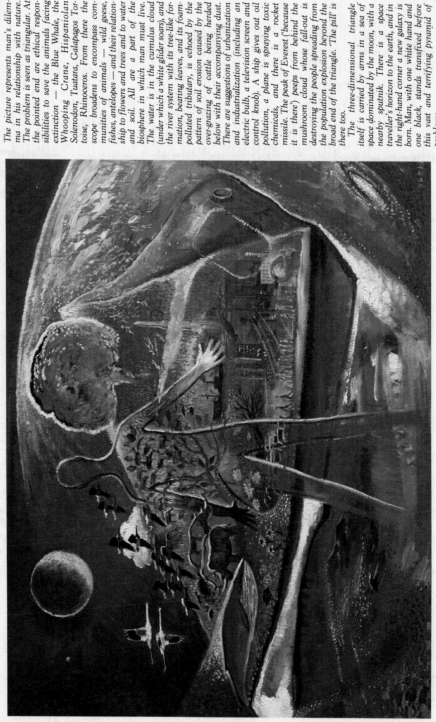

The natural world of man.
Sir Peter Scott

The picture represents man's dilemma in his relationship with nature. The problem is seen as triangular. At the pointed end are ethical responsibilities to save the animals facing extinction — the Blue Whale, *the* Whooping Crane, Hispaniolan Solenodon, Tuatara, Galapagos Tortoise, Rhinoceros. *From there the scope broadens to encompass communities of animals — wild geese, fishes, antelopes — and their relationship to flowers and trees and to water and soil. All are a part of the biosphere in which man must live. The water is in the cumulus cloud (under which a white glider soars), and the river system with its tree-like formation, bearing leaves, and its foam-polluted tributary, is echoed by the pattern of soil erosion caused by the over-grazing of cattle being herded below with their accompanying dust. There are suggestions of urbanization and industrialization (including an electric bulb, a television screen and control knob). A ship gives out oil pollution, a plane is spraying toxic chemicals, and there is a rocket missile. The peak of Everest ('because it is there') peeps from behind the mushroom cloud whose fall-out is destroying the people spreading from the population explosion beyond the broad end of the triangle. 'The pill' is there too.*

The three-dimensional triangle itself is carried by arms in a sea of space dominated by the moon, with a nearby sputnik. There is a space traveller's horizon to the earth, and in the right-hand corner a new galaxy is born. Man, with one white hand and one black, stands transfixed before this vast and terrifying pyramid of problems.

THE STATE OF THE ENVIRONMENT TODAY:

THE NEEDS FOR TOMORROW

By Nay Htun

DURING THE PAST 30 YEARS the world has witnessed unprecedented growth. As a result vast amounts of natural resources have been and continue to be consumed, and in the process critical life-support systems and the state of the environment are being affected. There is growing concern that these changes could have serious and irreversible consequences for planet earth.

The scale of change can be measured with a few stark statistics: every year 20 million hectares of arable land is lost; 12 million hectares of tropical forests are destroyed; 25 billion tonnes of top soil are washed away; and 3,000 billion tonnes of soil and rock are moved in mining operations.

At the same time, water consumption has increased from 3,000 cubic kilometres in 1980 to 3,750 in 1985. Commercial fuel consumption is now the equivalent of 7,500 million metric tonnes of oil, almost double the amount 20 years ago, and the number of motor vehicles has increased from 50 million in 1950 to 410 million in the early '80s. Most significantly, the population is now growing by more than a billion every 15 years, so that by the end of the century it will be six billion — double the number of people in 1960.

These awesome figures tend to numb the mind, but it is quite clear that planet earth has been subjected to tremendous misuse and abuse. It has been stripped, leveled, filled, extracted, dried, flooded and denuded of vegetation on a scale that stretches to the limit the earth's power to assimilate.

In this article I will offer a brief overview of the state of the air, water, soil and forests; describe some of the many technical, economic and institutional measures being undertaken to correct the degradation and reverse the trend; and finally suggest some of the measures that need to be taken to promote development activities that will improve not only standards of living but also the quality of life, by using resources rationally, and with minimal impact on the environment — in short sustainable development.

In conclusion I want to advocate strongly the imperative need to embody the ethical dimension of compassion, tolerance, respect for all forms of life, and responsible stewardship of the earth.

The state of the environment

An increasing amount of information and data on the environment is now available. In 1982 the United Nations Environment Programme, UNEP, undertook a detailed and comprehensive review of the state of the environment. UNEP also publishes annually State of the Environment Reports that focus on different topical issues. Similarly, Brown (1986) produces yearly State of the World reports. And recently the World Resources Institute (1986) provided an assessment of the resource base that supports the entire world's economy. In addition, at the national level an increasing number of countries issue state of the environment reports.

The atmosphere

There are a number of air quality crises confronting the world. These are 'acid rain' precipitation, the increase of 'greenhouse gases' and destruction of the ozone layer.

'Acid rain' is the phenomenon where sulphur and nitrogen oxides, released from the combustion of fossil fuels and natural sources such as volcanic eruptions are scavenged by clouds and cause rain and snow to become acidic. About 180 million tonnes of these oxides are emitted every year, and carried over distances of 1,000 km and more.

The death of lake fish in Scandinavia and North America has been directly attributed to the leaching of toxic metals from the soil. While there is as yet no unanimous agreement that acid rain is the cause of this or the large scale destruction of forests in Europe, there is growing acceptance that it is one of the main causes, either directly or indirectly by triggering other weakening mechanisms. Acid precipitation is also responsible for accelerated deteriorations of priceless buildings, monuments and statues. The rusting of ferrous metals and the need to repaint are often, thereby, increasing the economic costs as well as the cultural.

Turning to the build-up of 'greenhouse gases', there is now compelling evidence that increased concentrations of gases such as carbon dioxide, carbon monoxide, methane, nitrous oxides and chloroflurocarbons, which control the earth's ozone layer could lead to a climatic warming through the greenhouse effect. In terms of quantity, carbon dioxide build-up is by far the largest. Between 1950 and 1980 it increased at an average rate of four percent a year.

Basically, the presence of greenhouse gases produces an insulating effect. They permit higher energy solar radiation to reach the earth's surface. In turn the earth radiates low energy rays. Some are lost in outer space but some are absorbed by the greenhouse gases, which warm up the atmosphere.

This warming process has been understood since the 1930s and has been a matter of much earlier speculation. During the past decade more research has been undertaken and at the UNEP/WMO/ICSU Conference on Greenhouse Gases, Climatic Change and Associated Impacts held in 1985 in Villach, Austria, the international consensus was that if atmospheric carbon dioxide concentrations were to double, the global mean temperature would increase by 1.5 to 4.5 degrees Centigrade. Wind, ocean current and precipitation patterns would change, causing sea levels to rise between 20 and 140 cm., and many coastal cities will be under water. There will also be profound effects on global ecosystems, agriculture and water resources causing immense social and economic consequences.

Just as crucial is the damage being done to the ozone layer, which occurs high in the stratosphere. Ozone absorbs short wave-length ultra-violet radiation, letting only the far less harmful longer wave-length rays reach the earth. However, when the ozone concentration is depleted or the layer destroyed, more UV rays pass through the stratosphere.

The major substances which deplete the ozone layer are two nitrogen oxides, water molecules and chloroflurocarbons commonly used as aerosel can propellants and refrigerants. The response of human skin to sunlight is most pronounced at the higher wave-lengths, and the most common effect is sunburn, but two types of skin cancer can result, one of them often fatal.

An increase in the amount of ultra-violet rays reaching the earth's surface will also affect vegetation. The U.S. National Crop Loss Assessment Network reported that at a concentration of 0.12 parts per million of ozone, a peanut crop was 50 percent smaller than a similar crop grown under ideal conditions. Changes in stratospheric ozone would also affect heating rates, air movements, penetration of infra-red radiation and water vapour concentrations.

Water and its uses

The total volume of water is about 1,400 million km^3 and changes very little. However, more than 97 percent of the total is sea water. Only 0.01 percent is "fresh" and readily available. The remainder is locked in the polar ice caps, in depths of more than 75 meters, or in the atmosphere as water vapour. This relatively meagre quantity of available water is often wasted.

Accurate data for water withdrawals are not available, but rough estimates on total water use was about 3,000 km^3 in 1985. Irrigation accounted for 73 percent, followed by industry's 21 percent and 6 percent for domestic use.

The gross area under irrigation worldwide increased from about 28 million to 50 million hectares between 1960 and 1985. Despite this intensive use, irrigation is only 30-50 percent effective. Excessive use of ground water in relatively dry areas has depleted aquifers and improper design and management of irrigation systems have caused salinization, alkalination and waterlogging.

Industrial uses of water in developed countries have been decreasing in the last decade because of increased efficiency and recycling. In the U.S., Japan and

West Germany, for example, water is used in the plant at least twice before it is discharged. However in developing countries industrial water consumption rates have been increasing with industrial growth and there is an urgent need for conservation measures.

Public uses of water, for drinking, sanitation and sewage, although making up a small percent of the total, have very important effects on human health. Three out of five people in developing countries do not have easy access to safe drinking water and nearly 2 billion people are exposed to diseases by drinking contaminated water. As regards sanitation, three out of four people in the developing world do not have any kind of sanitation system.

Water pollution is a well-known problem. The inland waters of many countries are experiencing over-enrichment by nutrients from agricultural fertilizers and domestic sewage, causing heavy growths of algae. The widespread increase of nitrogenous fertilizers in many rivers and ground waters is also causing concern. Untreated sewage degrades the quality of the water and in most developing countries the coliform content is so high that it is unfit for human consumption.

With increasing industrialization, the quantity and variety of pollutants discharged have also increased. Although impressive efforts have been made and technical progress achieved in the treatment of industrial water pollution, there is growing concern about non-biodegradable toxic chemical pollutants that are in trace quantities, making them difficult to detect with conventional instruments and hard to remove from the water.

The productivity of the marine environment and its capacity to disperse pollutants depend on its physical and chemical properties, which are affected by sewage, agricultural chemicals, oil and metals. It has been estimated that about 25 billion tonnes of materials are added to the ocean each year, over 90 percent via rivers.

Coastal zone developments affect extensive areas of mangroves and coral reefs. Mangroves play an important part in the economics of tropical countries, and for millenia they have constituted a crucial habitat for many unique plants and animals. Mangrove ecosystems also support commercial fishing and provide living space for more than 2,000 species of fish, invertebrates and plants. Yet, globally less than 1 percent of the world's mangroves are officially protected.

Coral reefs are possibly the most productive ecosystems in the world. Although they occupy only 0.1 percent of the earth surface, about 10 percent of the world's fish catch is associated with the reefs. Also, coastal communities in the tropics derive much of their subsistence needs, security and cultural utility from coral reefs, which are now facing degradation from pesticides.

The state of the soil

The world at present has about 1.5 billion hectares of arable land under cultivation. It is estimated that each year about 25 billion tonnes of valuable top soil are lost. About 6 billion hectares, or 40 percent of the earth's land surface are desert, and every year from 5-7 million hectares of arable land become desert. The major causes are heavy grazing during droughts and overstocking, or population pressures which result in extreme subdivision and fragmentation of land holdings.

For irrigated lands the main desertification problems are waterlogging and salinization, which affect all regions of the world. Meanwhile forests and woodlands are lost through over-logging for fuel and timber, clearing for agriculture, fires and overgrazing. Since the affected areas are commonly watersheds, deforestation leads to increased run-off and flooding, accelerated water erosion and siltation, which often extend into adjacent lower-lying areas of land use.

By the year 2000, the WRI (1986) study reported, there would be about 0.5 hectare of cropland per person in the industrialized world, about 0.25 hectare in centrally planned economics and an average of 0.19 hectare in the developing countries. That means areas with the greatest need tend to have the least available land.

Among the types of soil degradation included in the process of desertification, erosion is one of the most widespread. Depending on local conditions, soil loss and new soil formation are approximately in balance at an erosion rate of 0.5 to 2 tonnes per hectare per year. Agriculture, especially on steep slopes, increases the rate substantially. Lost soil may be carried away by wind and water. One reason erosion is difficult to control is that many of its costly impacts occur miles away from the eroding field. Off-site effects of erosion include damage to fish and coral reefs, loss of hydropower potential, lower storage capacity in reservoirs, and increased need for dredging rivers and harbours. In the U.S. the off-site costs of erosion are estimated to be US$16 billion.

The rapid rise in the population is the immediate cause of deteriorating food-production systems. Growing populations have a fixed supply of arable land, but too often diminish its quality and quantity. As the demand for food increases, agriculture is extended onto marginal land and traditional techniques for keeping erosion in check and land productive, such as terracing, crop rotation and fallowing, are breaking down.

One indication of the rate of erosion is the size of the sedimentation loads of the Yangtse, Ganges, Amazon, Mississippi and Mekong rivers, which now total 3,883 million tonnes a year.

The death of forests and species

Tropical forests provide mankind with a wide range of benefits. They supply over half of the raw ingredients needed by the pharmaceutical industry; essential oils, latex, fibers, dyes, resins and gums; and protective watersheds that regulate water flows to more than a billion farmers downstream. Furthermore tropical forests are home to some 200 million people who rely on them for their fuel, food, shelter and animal fodder; and diverse species, 20 to 30 times greater than in temperate forests. According to the WRI (1986) report, about 1.7 million species have been indentified. A widely accepted minimum is 5 million and many scientists believe that the total could exceed 10 million. At least 75 percent of these species are estimated to occur in tropical zones.

The extinction of species has occured since the dawn of time, but the rate has accelerated alarmingly recently. Some have predicted that by the end of the century a further million species could be lost. A major reason is the destruction of habitats, particularly tropical forests. Deforestation is due to slash and burn farming, logging, cattle ranching, construction of hydroelectric dams, human settlements and highway construction. While there has been increased efforts recently to reforestation schemes, the rate of deforestation is five to 10 times greater. Also reforestation is primarily focused on single-species plantations, which have far less diversity than natural forests, often with non-indigenous trees for commercial use. It is estimated that annually about 12 million hectares of tropical forests are lost.

How can we improve the state of the environment?

The measures that have been undertaken are numerous and far ranging, using institutional, technical and economic approaches.

While in 1972 there were about a dozen countries with Ministries or Departments of the Environment, now almost all have some form of institutional means of managing the environment. In addition most countries have strengthened and revised environmental legislation and many have promulgated new ones to deal with emerging problems such as acid rain, toxic chemicals and hazardous wastes.

At the regional level an increasing number of organisations have been formed to enhance environmental cooperation. In Asia and the Pacific these include the ASEAN Expert Group on the Environment, the South Asia Cooperative Environment Programme, and the South Pacific Regional Environment Programme. The OECD's Environment Committee has a very active programme to foster cooperation among member states and, recently, the African Ministers for Environment met and launched the Cairo Plan of Action. Similar efforts have also been made in Latin America and the Caribbean. The need for regional cooperation is underscored by the 11 programmes of the UNEP Regional Seas Programme with participation of 120 countries.

At the international level, there are now more than 80 multilateral treaties available to protect the environment and wildlife and encourage the rational use of natural resources. These include the Convention on International Trade of Endangered Species and the 1980 World Conservation Strategy prepared by the International Union of Conservation of Nature and Natural Resources (IUCN)

Open-billed storks at Wat Phai Lom, near Bangkok in Thailand. The bird still exists because the breeding and feeding grounds of this species are within the sanctuary of a Buddhist temple.

Photo: T. Martorano

Illustration: Adrian Dyson

with the cooperation and financial assistance of UNEP and WWF and the collaboration of FAO and UNESCO.

Recognising the importance of environmental education, many if not most schools now include the subject in their curricula. An expanding array of teaching aids is being developed and used to promote environmental education. At the tertiary level the number of institutions offering courses on the environment has also increased appreciably. In Asia and the Pacific, for example, there are at least 248 institutions with courses related to the environment, and more are offering post-graduate courses.

The media has also played a significant role in increasing environmental awareness. Almost all newspapers regularly carry articles on the subject, and environmental accidents, such as Sveso, Bhopal, Chernobyl and the Rhine received extensive coverage.

This increase in awareness has prompted people to become interested in and concerned with environmental matters. One of the most significant developments in the past two decades has been the growing involvement of the public in protecting nature. Individuals and groups have formed associations to do something positive. These include the Chipko Movement to stop deforestation and the People's Forestry Movement of India to enlist the cooperation of villagers and plant a million trees and the 100 Million Trees Programme of Sri Lanka.

Technical measures available to treat gaseous, liquid and solid wastes are many, and technology is rarely the constraint to pollution control. The growth of pollution control services has been very pronounced in industrialized countries. For example in the U.S.A. the total expenditure for pollution control in 1979 was about US$56 billion, more than 2 percent of GNP. By 1988 this is expected to rise to US$160 billion. In Japan the investment in anti-pollution measures increased from about US$12 billion in 1970 to US$64 billion in 1975 and now averages US$30 billion per year.

Recently there has been an increase in the use of low and non-waste technologies in industry to encourage production with less and less dangerous waste, with raw materials and energy used more economically, and less-polluting end products.

Economic and fiscal measures are also being used to encourage environmental management and discourage pollution. These include tax rebates or subsidies for pollution-control equipment or the application of the Polluter Pays Principle adopted by OECD countries.

The needs for tomorrow

With population growth there will be more people with increasing aspirations for higher standards of living and an improved quality of life. The demand for natural resources and environmental amenities will increase accordingly and so will the potential impacts on environmental quality, if appropriate policies and strategies are not enacted. The challenge will be to meet these expectations while ensuring that the functioning and integrity of the ecosystem, particularly the critical life-support systems, are not irreversibly damaged.

There is now a growing acceptance of the concept of sustainable development as a means to meet this challenge, and the measures that need to be taken.

The Ministries and Departments of the Environment that have been established need strengthening. Many of them are relatively new, and resources — financial and personal — commensurate to the task, should be made available. The trend in an increasing number of countries which require development activities to be subject to an environmental impact assessment (EIA) process needs to be emulated in those countries which do not. Equally important is the establishment of policy directives to ensure that the EIA process be applied at the earliest feasible planning stage of any project, rather than when designs are completed and construction begins, when any changes will be time-consuming, costly and often unfeasible. The early application of the process will promote and facilitate the adoption of alternate sites, raw material use, manufacturing processes, products and such, with less impact on the environment and more efficient use of natural resources. To date, while the EIA process has been increasingly applied, it has been primarily aimed at the project level. To ensure the maximum effect it should be directed at the programme and planning levels as well.

The development plans of a country are generally based on economic parameters and indicators such as GNP and GDP. The wealth of a country is now measured by the quantity of minerals, fossil fuels, industrial and agricultural outputs. To promote sustainable development there is a need to apply the concept of "environmental accounting" as proposed by Dr. M. K. Tolba, the Executive Director of UNEP. This makes the quality of the water and air, the amount of top soil, the area of biosphere reserves needed for genetic diversity, and other ecological factors part of a country's patrimony.

When environmental institutions were established 10 to 15 years ago by a majority of countries, the major focus was on pollution control, since pollutants from industry, transportation and homes were visibly a cause of environmental degradation. Now, however, there is a growing recognition that this is not enough. There is also a need to consider preventive measures in the use of resources and the secondary and tertiary impacts of environmental degredation, particularly those affecting social and cultural conditions. There is an imperative need for an integrated approach to ensure that the people who are trained in pollution control are also educated in the broader aspects of environmental management. Without them it will not be possible to conceive, plan and implement the integration of environmental considerations for sustainable development.

While countries have enacted environmental legislation, it has not yet been vigorously enforced due to lack of personnel, finances and information on the most cost-effective solutions. These constraints are most prevalent in developing

Nature as seen and portrayed by people of northern Thailand in this example of folk art. Some recent examples of this craft portray people running in all directions from bombs dropping from airplanes instead of the harmonious nature here.

Photo: T. Martorano

countries. Greater enforcement, therefore, should be accompanied by incentives and assistance to encourage adoption of environmental management.

During the past two decades the public has been provided with accounts of the extent of the degradation of planet earth. They must continue to be supplied with credible information. This should include reports on the increasing number of activities that are being undertaken to improve the state of the environment, to show that solutions can be found, so that people do not feel hopeless and despondent.

There is a recognition that for any activity to yield maximum benefits there must be a focus at grass-root levels. There must be people participation with a strategy that accepts the role of the individual.

The attitudes and actions of a person can have very important impacts on environmental quality and natural resource use, as an example for others. So can the sum of individual attitudes and actions have a very telling impact. Hence it is imperative to motivate and orient all people, most specifically the individual, to place a higher premium on ethical values. Compassion and tolerance towards all living beings; respect for all forms of life; harmony with nature rather than the arrogance to conquer it; responsible stewardship of nature for the benefits of present and future generations; less profligate use of resources — these are some of the fundamental attitudes and practices that need to be strengthened.

The Lord Buddha recognised these ethical principles and taught and practiced them Himself over two millennia ago. These principles apply even more today. The need for today and tomorrow is for the individual to be aware of the fundamental importance of environmental ethics and practice them.

Nay Htun, Ph.D., a Buddhist, is Regional Director and Representative for Asia and the Pacific of the United Nations Environment Programme. Prior to joining UNEP in 1976, he was Professor of Environmental Engineering at the Asian Institute of Technology as well as working for a multinational energy company. His contribution here is written in a personal capacity.

References

Brown, L.R. and others (1986). State of the World. A Worldwatch Institute Report on Progress Towards a Sustainable Society, W.W. Norton & Company, New York, London.

United Nations Environment Programme, UNEP (1982). The World Environment 1972-1982. Ed. by M.W. Holdgate, M. Kassas, G.F. White. United Nations Environment Programme.

UNEP/WMO/ICSU (1985). An Assessment of the Role of Carbon Dioxide and other Greenhouse Gases in Climate Variations and Associated Impacts. WMO, Geneva.

UNEP (1986). Directory of Tertiary Level Institutions Offering Environmental Education and Training Courses in Asia and Pacific Region. UNEP Regional Office for Asia and the Pacific, Bangkok.

World Resources Institute (1986). An Assessment of the Resource Base that Supports the Global Economy. Basic Books Inc., New York.

THE BUDDHIST PERCEPTION OF NATURE PROJECT

By Nancy Nash

"The world grows smaller and smaller, more and more inter-dependent...today more than ever before life must be characterized by a sense of Universal Responsibility, not only nation to nation and human to human, but also human to other forms of life."

His Holiness The Dalai Lama

BUDDHIST PERCEPTION OF NATURE, a project created to improve awareness, attitudes, and actions concerning the natural environment, took root with this statement by His Holiness The Dalai Lama during the course of an interview in 1979, and has been nurtured at every step with inspiration and support from the world's foremost Buddhist leader.

Our work involves researching, assembling, and putting to use as educational tools, Buddhist teachings about man's responsibilities to the natural world and all living beings. Many of the lessons from Buddhist literature and art date back more than 2,500 years, but they are as valid today as they have ever been, and capable of reaching out in many modern forms in contemporary society. Buddhism in fact, was selected for the pilot project in new perspectives for environmental education because it is an ancient, enduring philosophy, embodying strongly themes of awareness and compassion for all life.

The faith is also influential in many parts of Asia that have unique and endangered species of animals, plants and habitats, and has been demonstrated to have a direct, beneficial effect in saving some species of wildlife and threatened habitats.

The conservation effect for the most part may be described as passive protection. Animals inhabiting the grounds of temples, for example, have automatic sanctuary for Buddhist faithful; in Thailand rules for monks living in forest monasteries are so strict that their areas are naturally well cared for. Tibet, by all accounts, was until the culture was disrupted by the Chinese takeover in 1950, a land where people and wildlife lived together in extraordinary harmony.

The environmental crisis we face today, however, needs active help, and the world's estimated 500 million Buddhists can make a major, positive impact by becoming active conservationists.

A focus on human, spiritual and cultural values in no way ignores the role of science, which itself is also part of the human cultural world. Our project recognises that science is essential, first to set priorities for the work, and to persuade educated leaders and decision-makers. Then our best scientific minds are needed to help rectify the ecological disasters we face resulting from ignorance, greed, and lack of respect for the earth.

Objective scientists are the first professionals to point out and prove that the earth's capacity to support life is clearly being reduced at the time it is needed most — as rising human numbers, expectations, and consumption make increasingly heavy demands.

But science outlines the state of the earth. Religion and cultural traditions are the repositories of human values, and many people today feel it is only with aroused personal and social values that we may begin to deal with our current problems in a way which will benefit life on earth now, and in the future.

The importance of excellence in scholarship cannot be over-estimated in a project of this kind, and we are fortunate that, from the commencement of work, research has been under the direction of highly respected institutions, and carried out by superb scholars.

The Council for Religious and Cultural Affairs and the Information Office of His Holiness The Dalai Lama have provided direction for Mahayana studies. For Theravada traditions, work has been guided by Wildlife Fund Thailand in association with experts from the Thai Ministry of Education and Thammasat University. Our chief scholars — Dr. Chatsumarn Kabilsingh in Bangkok, and Venerable Karma Gelek Yuthok in Dharamsala, India — and their colleagues assisting with research, compiling and translating, have done a remarkable job involving a vast literature and history, in a very short space of time.

Deputy Minister for Education in His Holiness The Dalai Lama's Kashag (Cabinet) Lodi Gyaltsen Gyari is *Buddhist Perception of Nature's* Tibetan Coordinator, and our Thai Coordinator is Mr. Sirajit Waramontri, Member of the Board of Trustees of Wildlife Fund Thailand. Both have given this project valuable time, energy, and creative talent to launch the work, and keep it going with the momentum resulting in this book — the first of many educational products planned.

Tibetan and Thai Buddhists have undertaken the initial work for the simple reason that they were sympathetic and influential individuals willing to take on the burden of the tasks. Contacts with other Buddhist communities and countries have come about in the normal course of events and all are welcome to participate.

Because of the global concerns of conservation, this project from the beginning was envisioned as important, first among Buddhists, but also as an adaptable blueprint for research and achievement for similar projects involving other faiths and cultural traditions.

Buddhist Perception of Nature aims to provide samples of the project design and educational materials to all groups, governmental and private, Buddhist and other faiths, wishing to study and use them. All of us involved with the work are therefore touched, and inspired by the interest already shown by individuals and groups from many different parts of the world, and different religions and cultural traditions, who find the project not only a viable response to the ecological problems today, but also an element in a much-needed renaissance of environmental ethics.

Nancy Nash, originator and International Coordinator of the Buddhist Perception of Nature project, is an American, a Christian, and author of more than 100 book and magazine articles and chapters about wildlife, nature conservation and culture.

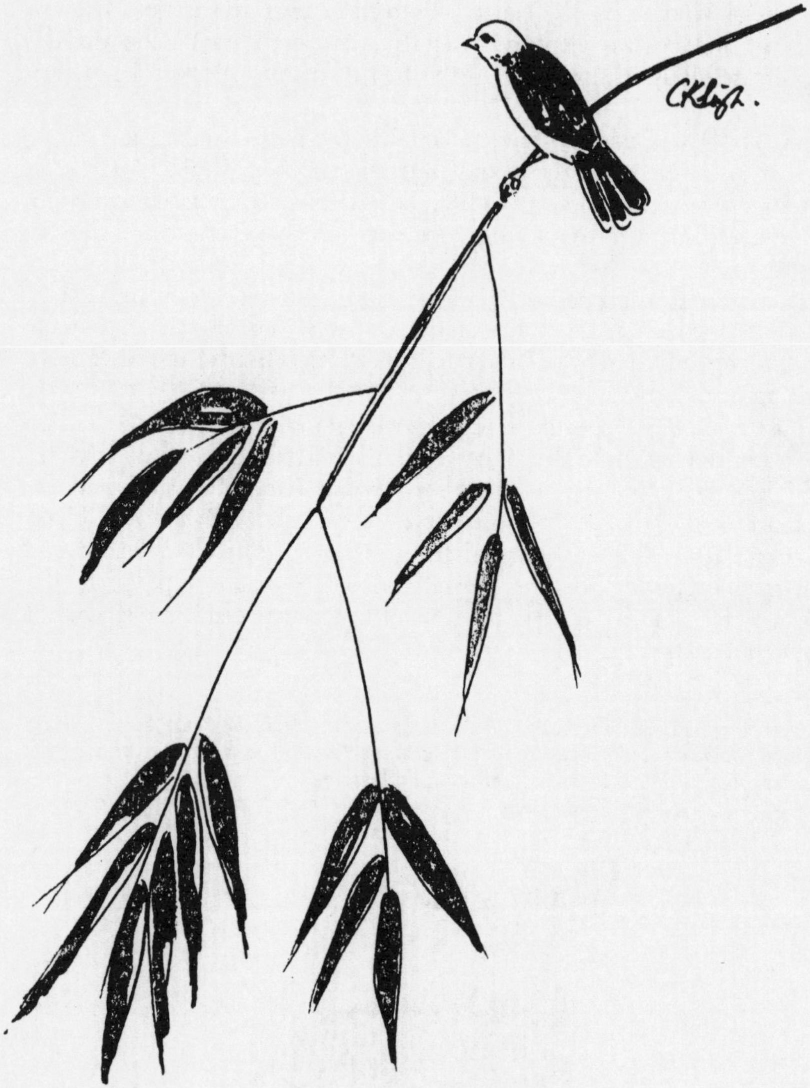

གོང་ས་སྐྱབས་མགོན་སྐུ་ཕྲེང་བཅུ་བཞི་པ་ཏཱ་ལའི་བླ་མ་བསྟན་འཛིན་རྒྱ་མཚོ་མཆོག་གི་
གསུང་འཕྲིན།

The Rolex Awards for Enterprise

དཔར་བསྒྲུས་དབང་ཆ།

ནང་ཆོས་ཚོགས་ནས་རང་བྱུང་ཁམས་ལ་ལྟ་ཕྱོགས་ཀྱི་ལས་འགུལ།

དཀར་ཆགས།

༧༥། ནང་ཆོས་ནས་རང་བྱུང་ཁམས་ཕྱོགས་བརྟ་ཚུལ་ཞིབ་པའི་དཔེ་དེབ་དང་། ལས་འགུལ་འདི་བཞིན་འགྲོ་བ་མིས་འདོད་ཆམ་གྱིས་རང་བཞིན་གྱི་ཁོར་ཡུག་སྲུང་སྐྱོབ་ཕྱོགས་གཏོར་སྐྱོན་བྱུགས་ཆེར་ཡོང་བཞིན་པ་བཀག་འགོད་ཐབ་ཐབས་སུ་སློབ་གསོ་ཐེལ་བའི་ཡག་ཆེའི་ལས་འགུལ་གསར་པ་ཞིག་ཡིན།

ལོ་ཉིས་སྟོང་ཞ་བརྒྱའི་ཇོན་གྱི་ལམ་ལུགས་དང་། སློབ་གསོའི་ལམ་སྟོན་གསར་ཐེལ་བྱས་པར་གཅིག་བྱས་ཞ་ཡ་མཚན་མདོག་ཁ་པོ་རེད། རྩ་དོན་འདི་བཞིན་གལ་ཆེར་བརྩེན་གཞུང་དང་། མིར་གྱི་ཚོགས་ཁག་བཅས་ནས་འགན་འཁུར་གྱིས་རང་བྱུང་ཁམས་སྲུང་སྐྱོབ་ཀྱིས་ལས་འགུལ་བྱས་པ་ནས་མི་ལོ་བཅུ་ཕྲག་གཉིས་ཙམ་འགྲོ་གི་ཡོད་པ་མ་ཟད། དེང་གི་འཚར་ཡོངས་ཁྱབ་ཏུ་ཁས་ལེན་བྱེད་བཞིན་ཡོད། དེ་འདྲ་སོང་ཙང་དེང་དུས་ཀྱི་དཀའ་ངལ་གྱི་རྒྱ་རྐྱེན་འདི་སེལ་ཐབས་སུ་ང་རང་ཚོའི་བསམ་བློའི་ནང་ཞ་རབས་ཀྱི་བསླབ་བྱ་རྣམས་ལག་བསྟར་གང་གི་ཐྱིར་བྱེད་ཀྱི་མེད་དམ། རྒྱུ་མཚན་ནི། ཁོར་ཡུག་སྲུང་སྐྱོབ་ཀྱི་ལས་འགུལ་ལས་དེར་གཏོར་སྐྱོན་གཏོང་མཁན་ཚོས་རྒྱ་ཆེ་བ་ཡོད་པར་སོང་ཙང་དུ་སྔར་ཁོར་ཡུག་སྲུང་སྐྱོབ་ཀྱི་ལས་འགུལ་གྱི་དཀའ་ངལ་སེལ་ཐུབ་ཀྱི་མེད།

ཁོར་ཡུག་སྲུང་སྐྱོབ་ཀྱི་ལས་འགུལ་འདི་ཕལ་ཆེར་ཞ་དྲག་གིས་དཀའ་ངལ་འཕྲད་པ་ལས་བྱུང་བ་ ཞི ཡིན་གཞིས་དེ་ཡང་སྐྱིས་ལུགས་ཚན་རིག་ཕྱོགས་ཀྱི་དཀའ་ངལ་ལ་དམིགས་ཏེ་འཛུགས་བསྐྲུན་ཟ་ཚོགས་པའི་ལམ་ནས་ལས་འགུལ་ཐེལ་ཐབས་བྱ་རྒྱུ་དེ་རེད། འོན་ཀྱང་ད་ཡོད་རང་བྱུང་ཁམས་དང་། རང་བྱུང་གཏེར་སོགས་ལ་གནོད་འཚབ་བྱས་པ་དང་། ད་ཆ་རྒྱ་ཆེར་བྱེད་བཞིན་ཡོར་ཀསལ་སྲོད་ཡང་དག་པར་བྱེད་ཐུབ་མེད།

དེའི་རྒྱུ་མཚན་གཅིག་ནི། སྲོག་ཆགས་དང་། རྩི་ཤིང་ཟ་ཚོགས་པར་གནོད་འཚབ་ཛི་ཆེར་བྱེད་པ་ཤིས་བཞིན་དུ་དེ་ལས་སྐྱོབ་པའི་ཐབས་སུ་དཔལ་འབྱོར་སོགས་ཀྱི་དཀའ་ངལ་ལ་བརྟེན་ནས་ལས་འགུལ་འདི་བཞིན་འགོ་ཚུགས་ཐུབ་མེད། ཡང་རྒྱུ་མཚན་གཞན་ཞིག་ནི། དེར་དོ་སྣང་མ་བྱས་པར་དེ་སྔར་ལུས་རྗེས་ཛ་དྲག་ཕྱུགས་ཆེ་འགྲོ་ཀྱབས་འ་འདྲ་མ་འདུས་པའི་སྐབས་སུ་ཕྱི་བུར་ལས་འགུལ་རྩོམ་དགོས་པའི་རྐྱེན་གྱི་རེད།

རྒྱུ་མཚན་གཙོ་བོ་ནི། ཛི་སྟར་སྲུང་སྐྱོབ་བྱེད་པའི་གནས་ལུགས་ཉམས་ལེན་བྱེད་པའི་ཕྱོགས་དང་། དེ་བཞིན་དཔལ་འབྱོར་དང་། ཡར་རྒྱས། སྨ་མཐུད་སྟོན་ཕྱོག་འདེབས་ལས། མདོར་ན་སྟོང་གསུམ་གྱི་སྟོང་ཆེན་པོ་འཇིག་རྟེན་ཁམས་གནས་པའི་སྲོག་རྫོར་བརྟེན་ནན་ཏན་བཟོད་པ་ཞིག་ཡིན།

གདམས་ངག་འདི་ནི་ད་ལྟ་དང་། མ་འོངས་པའི་མི་རབས་རྣམས་ཀྱི་བདེ་རྩར་གལ་གནད་ཤིན་ཏུ་ཆེ་བའང་། དེ་ལ་སུས་ཀྱང་དོ་སྣང་བྱས་མེད། ནང་ཆོས་ཕྱོག་ནས་རང་བྱུང་ཁམས་སྲུང་སྐྱོབ་ཀྱི་སྟ་བ་འདི་ནི་རིག་གཞུང་འདྲ་མིན་དང་། སྨྲི་ཚོགས་དང་། མི་སེར་སོ་སོས་དཀའ་ངལ་དེ་ལས་རྩོག་ཐབས་ཀྱི་རྒྱས་པའི་ཕྱོག་ནན་ཏན་བཟོད་ཀྱི་ཡོད།

མ་འོངས་པའི་དཔལ་འབྱོར་དང་། ཚན་རིག་གི་གནད་དོན་ཐོག་གལ་ཆེར་འགྱུར་ཡོད་སྟབས་རྣམ་པར་བྱང་ཆུབ་པའི་གཞུང་དང་། ཚོང་དོན་དབུ་གཙོ་རྣམ་པས་ལས་འགུལ་དེར་ཞུགས་དགོས་པའི་འབོད་བསྐུལ་བྱས་ནའང་། ཁོང་ཚོས་རྒྱ་མཚན་དེ་ཙམ་ལ་དགོངས་ནས་ལག་ལེན་བསྟར་མི་ཡོང་སྙམ། རང་བྱུང་ཁམས་གཏོར་བཤིགས་བྱེད་པ་དང་། དེ་སྲུང་སྐྱོབ་བྱེད་མཁན་ཚོས་རྒྱ་མཚན་རྩ་ཚིགས་ལ་སྟོས་ཏེ་བྱེད་ཀྱི་ཡོད་པ་མངོན་གསལ་དོད་པོ་རེད། ཡོངས་ལ་ཏཱ་ལའི་བླ་མ་མཆོག་ནས་དེའི་ཐོག་གསུང་འཕྲིན་བཀའ་སློབ་གནང་བ་ལྟར། འཛམ་གླིང་སྣོད་བཅུད་ལ་གཏོར་སྐྱོན་གཏོང་བ་དེ་ནི་འགྲོ་བ་མིའི་འདོད་ཧམ་གྱི་རང་བཞིན་ལ་བརྟེན་ནས་བྱུང་བ་ཞིག་རེད། དེ་དང་དེ་བཞིན་གྱི་འགྲོ་བ་མིས་སེམས་ཅན་གཞན་ལ་གུས་བརྩེ་མེད་པའི་རྐྱེན་གྱི་གོམས་གཤིས་དེ་ཉམས་བརླག་འགྲོ་བ་ཡིན། ཞེས་བཀའ་སློབ་གནང་ཡོད།

རང་བྱུང་ཁམས་སྲུང་སྐྱོབ་བྱེད་མཁན་འགའ་ཤས་ཀྱིས་རང་ཉིད་དངོས་སུ་ནགས་གཞིབ་སོགས་གནས་དབེན་པའི་ཕྱོགས་སུ་བསྐྱོད་མ་ཐུབ་ནའང་། དེར་བསྐྱོད་ཐུབ་མཁན་གྱི་ལྟ་མཛུབ་གཞན་ལ་རོགས་ཕན་བྱེད་ཀྱི་ཡོད། ཚོང་པ་སོགས་རང་ཉིད་ཀྱི་འཚོ་ལས་ཀྱི་ཁེ་ཕན་ལ་སྟོས་པ་དང་། དེ་བཞིན་ཕྱུ་རྒྱུ་ཆོས་སེམས་ཅན་ལ་དགའ་སེམས་ཡོད་པའི་དབང་གི་ཁོང་ཚོའི་སེམས་ཅན་རྣམས་སྲུང་སྐྱོབ་བྱེད་དགོས་ཀྱི་ཡོད་ཅེས་ཟད་གར་བཏོང་ དེ་སྲུང་སྐྱོབ་བྱེད་ཀྱི་ཡོད།

ཚན་རིག་པ་འགའ་ཞིག་ལོ་ལོའི་སློབ་ཚན་ཐོག་ཚད་ལྡན་མཁས་པ་ཚོས་ལས་འགུལ་དེར་དོ་སྣང་བྱེད་དགོས་པ་ནི། སེམས་ཅན་རྣམས་ཀྱི་རིགས་ཀྱི་འབྱུང་ཁུངས་སོགས་འདྲ་མིན་ལ་སྟོས་ཏེ་བྱེད་ཀྱི་ཡོད། ངས་ཤེས་འཚོར་བྱུང་བའི་ནང་ཚན་རིག་པའི་ཁོངས་ནས་གཅན་གཟན་གྱི་རིགས་ལ་ཉམས་ཞིབ་པ་རྣམས་ཀྱི་ལས་དོན་དེར་མཁྱེན་ཡོན་རྩེ་ཕུད་ཅན་ཚོས་རང་བྱུང་ཁམས་སྲུང་སྐྱོབ་ཀྱི་ལས་འགུལ་བྱེད་ཀྱི་ཡོད།

ད་ལྟའི་འཛམ་གླིང་འདི་བཞིན་ད་ཡོད་བཞིན་གནས་ཐབས་སུ་བྱུགས་རྒྱུད་རིང་ཕོས་བཅོས་ཐབས་སྣ་ཚོགས་ཡོད་ཁོངས། ནང་པའི་ཆོས་ནས་གསུངས་པའི་བསླབ་ཚིག་རྣམས་དེ་ཁོངས་ཡོད། དེ་ལས་གལ་ཆེ་བ་དེའི་སྐོར་ཤེས་ཡོན་སློབ་གསོ་སྤེལ་ཐབས་དེ་ཡིན།

ནང་ཆོས་དང་། རང་བྱུང་ཁམས་ཀྱི་སྲུང་སྐྱོབ་ཅེས་པའི་ལས་འགུལ་འདི་ཁོངས་རྩོམ་དེབ་འདི་བཞིན་རང་བྱུང་ཁམས་སྲུང་སྐྱོབ་བྱེད་མཁན་གྱི་ནང་པའི་ས་ཁུལ་ཙམ་མ་ཡིན་པར་འཛམ་གླིང་ནང་རང་བྱུང་ཁམས་ལ་གཏོར་སྐྱོན་འགྲོ་བཞིན་པའི་ས་ཁུལ་ཚང་མར་གལ་ཆེར་འགྱུར་ཡོད།

དཔེ་དེབ་འདིའི་ནང་ཐ་ན་རང་ཉིད་ཀྱི་ཁྱིམ་ཚང་དང་། དེ་བཞིན་རྒྱ་ཆེར་སློབ་འཁྲིད་དང་། དབུ་འཁྲིད་ཚོས་ཀྱང་དེ་སྲུང་སྐྱོབ་བྱེད་དགོས་སྐོར་རང་བྱུང་ཁམས་སྲུང་སྐྱོབ་ཀྱི་སློབ་སྟོན་ཆ་ཚང་བཀོད་ཡོད། དཔེ་དེབ་འདི་བཞིན་གོ་སྒྲིག་བྱེད་ཕྱོགས་སུ་རང་བྱུང་ཁམས་སྲུང་སྐྱོབ་བྱེད་དགོས་པ་གལ་ཆེ་ཡིན་ཚུལ་དང་། རིག་གཞུང་། ཁས་ལེན་གྱི་སེམས་གཤིས། བརྩེ་སྐྱོད་མཁྱེན་རྟ་དངས་པོ་རིམ་བཞིན་ཆ་ཚང་དཔོད་ཡོད།

ཀྱི་ཞབས་མཁས་དབང་ཆེན་ལུ་མན་ཀ་ཐིལ་སིང་གིས་རང་བྱུང་ཁམས་སྲུང་སྐྱོབ་སྐོར་ནང་ཚོས་ཀྱི་བསླབ་བྱ་དང་། མཁས་དབང་ནི་ཀྲན་གྱིས་ད་ལྟའི་ཁོར་ཡུག་གི་གནས་སྟངས་བཅས་མཁས་པའི་རྣམ་དཔྱོད་ཀྱི་གྲུ་ཚལ་ལས་འདྲངས་པའི་རྩོམ་རིགས་དེ་དག་གིས་དཔེ་དེབ་འདིའི་གོ་དོན་གསལ་པོ་རྫོགས་ལྡན་ཀྱི་ཡོད། རང་བྱུང་ཁམས་སྲུང་སྐྱོབ་དེ་དུས་དང་རྣམ་པ་ཀུན་ཏུ་རང་ཉིད་ཀྱི་སེམས་སྤྱོལ་དུ་འགྱུར་བ་ན། མི་ཚེའི་ཟླས་ཚོད་ཀྱང་ཞིགས་སུ་འགྲོ་བ་ཡིན། ནང་པའི་ཆོས་ནས་གསུངས་པའི་བདེ་སྐྱིད་དང་། ཁོར་ཡུག་སྲུང་སྐྱོབ་ཀྱི་རྩ་བ་ནི། དེང་དུས་ཁོར་ཡུག་འཛིན་སྐྱོང་སྲིད་བྱུས་ནང་མངོན་གསལ་དོད་དུ་འགྲོ་གི་ཡོད།

ནང་ཆོས་ནང་། རང་བྱུང་ཁམས་སྲུང་སྐྱོབ་ཀྱི་ལས་འགུལ་འདི་བཞིན་འགོ་ཚུགས་པ་ནས། དེ་དང་འབྲེལ་བ་ཡོད་པ་དེར་ངོས་རང་དགའ་སྤྲོབས་ཆེན་པོ་བསྐྱེད་བྱུང་། ཕྱི་ལོ་ ༡༩༧༩ ལོར་ལས་འགུལ་འགོ་བཙུགས་མཁན་ནན་ལི་ཝེབ་འཛམ་གླིང་གཅན་གཟན་མ་དངུལ་བསྡུ་གསོག་ཀྱི་སློབ་སྟོན་པ་བྱེད་བཞིན་པའི་སྐབས་རང་བྱུང་སྲུང་སྐྱོབ་པ་ཚོས་འཛམ་གླིང་ཆོས་ལུགས་ཁག་ནས་རོགས་མགོན་ཞུ་དགོས་ཀྱི་རེད་གསུངས། ཁོང་ནས་རྒྱ་ནག་དང་འབྲེལ་བ་བཟོ་ཐབས་ཀྱི་བསམ་ཚུལ་བརྗོད་པ་ལྟར། རྒྱ་ནག་དང་འབྲེལ་བ་བཟོས་གནང་། ལས་འགུལ་དེའི་ཐོག་ལོ་མང་ཕྱག་ལས་གནང་མཐར་ཁོང་ལ་ཐུ་ཏྲམ་ཟན་ཏ་ཞེས་མཚན་འདོགས། དེ་རྗེས་ཁོང་སྟོང་ཀོང་དུ་འཛམ་གླིང་གཅན་གཟན་དངུལ་གསོག་ཀྱི་སྒྲིག་འཛུགས་ཤིག་ཀྱང་རོགས་མགོན་ཞུས་ཡོད།

མཐར་ཕྱི་ལོ་ ༡༩༨༥ ལོར་ཁོར་ཡུག་སྲུང་སྐྱོབ་ལས་འགུལ་འདི་བཞིན་འཆར་འགོད་བཞིན་དབུ་འཁྲིད་གནང་། ལོ་གཉིས་ནང་ལས་འགུལ་འདིས་ནང་ཆོས་ཀྱི་བསླབ་བྱ་ན ས་རང་བྱུང་ཁམས་ལ་མིའི་འགན་དབང་ཇི་ཡོད་གསལ་པོ་སྟོན་ཐུབ་པ་བྱུང་ཡོད་པ་མ་ཟད། ཁོར་ཡུག་ཐོག་ཀུན་སྤྱོད་འཕྱིར་སྐྱངས་ཐོག་ལའང་མི་མང་གི་སེམས་འཁུར་ཆེ་རུ་སོང་ཡོད།

རྩ་བའི་ཁོར་ཡུག་སྲུང་སྐྱོབ་ཐོག་ཀུན་སྤྱོད་འཕྱིར་སྐྱངས་རང་ཉིད་ཀྱི་མི་ཚེ་དང་། ལས་ཀའི་ཐོག་གལ་ཆེ་པོ་ཞིག་ཆགས་ཡོད། དེར་བརྟེན་ཕྱུག་གི་ཟླན་མིང་དང་། དེའི་དམིགས་ཡུལ་ནང་ཁོར་ཡུག་ཐོག་ཀུན་སྤྱོད་འཕྱིར་སྐྱངས་ཤུགས་ཆེ་གསལ་ཡོད་པར་ངོས་རང་དགའ་སྤྲོབས་ཞེ་དྲག་བྱུང་།

༧གོང་ས་ཏཱ་ལའི་བླ་མ་མཆོག་ནང་པ་ཙམ་མ་ཡིན་པར་འཛམ་གླིང་ཐང་ཡོངས་བརྩི་ཞུ་སའི་ཆོས་སྲིད་ཀྱི་དབུ་འཁྲིད་ཡང་དག་པ་ཞིག་ཡིན། ཁོང་གིས་ལས་འགུལ་འདི་འགོ་ཚུགས་པ་ནས་ད་བར་བཀའ་སློབ་རྒྱུན་སྐོར་བཀའ་དྲིན་ཆེ་བ་བཞིན། ང་ཚོ་ཆོས་ལུགས་གཞན་གྱི་དབུ་འཁྲིད་རྣམས་ཀྱིས་ཀྱང་༧གོང་ས་ཏཱ་ལའི་བླ་མའི་ཕྱུག་གི་ཟླན་མིང་དང་གསུངས་པའི་ཁོར་ཡུག་ཐོག་ཀུན་སྤྱོད་འཕྱིར་སྐྱངས་ཀྱི་གསུང་འབྲེལ་ལ་དཔེ་མཚོན་གནང་རོགས་ཞེས་རེ་བསྐུལ་ཞུ་གི་ཡོད།

རང་བྱུང་སྣོད་ཁམས་ལ་སྲུང་སྐྱོབ་དགོས་པའི་གསུང་འཕྲིན།

༄༅། །ང་ཚོས་ཤེས་གསལ་ལྟར། འགྲོ་བ་མིའི་ཁྱད་ནོར་རྣམས་ལ་རྩ་སྲུང་མི་བྱེད་པའི་མིའི་བྱ་སྤྱོད་ཀྱིས་འཛམ་གླིང་ས་སྟེང་གི་ཞི་བདེ་དང་སྲོག་ཆགས་རྣམས་རྒྱུན་གནས་མི་ཐུབ་པའི་ཉེན་ཁ་བཟོས་ཡོད་པ་རེད།

རང་བྱུང་གི་བཀོད་པ་དང་། ངེ་དག་གི་བདག་འབྲས་བཅུད་ནོར་རྣམས་ཀྱི་གཏེར་བཅོམ་ནི་། མི་ཤེས་པ་དང་། འདོད་ཛམས། སྲོག་ཆགས་ལ་རྩ་མཐོང་མེད་པ་བཅས་ལས་བྱུང་བ་ཞིག་རེད། རྩ་མཐོང་མེད་པའི་གཤིས་སྤྱོད་འདི་འགྲོ་བ་མིའི་མི་རབས་ཐོག་ཁྱབ་གདལ་དུ་འགྲོ་བཞིན་ཡོད་པས། གལ་ཏེ་འཛམ་གླིང་གི་ཞི་བདེ་ཞེས་པ་དེ་དངོས་བདེན་གྱི་གནས་ཚུལ་ཞིག་ཏུ་མ་གྱུར་པ་དང་། རང་བྱུང་ཁམས་ཀྱི་གཏེར་བཅོམ་ད་ཡོད་ཀྱི་གོམ་འགྲོས་དེ་འདི་མུར་གནས་ན། འབྱུང་འགྱུར་གྱི་མི་རབས་རྣམས་ནས་ཉམས་རྒུད་ཀྱི་ཆེར་སོང་ཟིན་པའི་གླིང་སྣོད་ཅིག་ལ་བརྒྱུད་འཛིན་བདག་དབང་བྱ་དགོས་སུ་གྱུར་ངེས་རེད། རང་རེའི་ཕ་མེས་རྣམས་ནས་འཛམ་གླིང་འདི་ནོར་བཅུད་ཀྱིས་ཕྱུག་ཅིང་། དགོས་འདོད་འཛད་མེད་འཛོ་བ་ཞིག་ཏུ་མྱོང་གནང་བྱུང་ཡོད་པ་དེ་ལྟར་རེད།

འདས་པའི་དུས་སུ་སྐྱེ་བོ་མང་པོ་ཞིག་ནས་རང་བྱུང་ཁམས་ཀྱི་དངོས་པོ་རྣམས་ལ་ཇི་ཙམ་ལོངས་སྤྱད་ཀྱང་། འཛད་མཐའ་མེད་པའི་རང་བཞིན་ཞིག་ཏུ་གནས་པ་མཐོང་གི་ཡོད་ཀྱང་། ད་ཆ་རང་བྱུང་ཁམས་ལ་བདག་སྐྱོད་གཅེས་སྐྱོང་ལེགས་པོ་ཞིག་མ་བྱས་ན་དེ་ལྟར་གནས་མི་ཐུབ་པ་ང་ཚོས་ཤེས་གསལ་རེད།

མི་ཤེས་པའི་དབང་ལས་འདས་པའི་དུས་སུ་གཏོར་བཅོམ་བྱུང་ཟིན་པ་རྣམས་ལ་བཟོད་བསྲན་བྱ་རྒྱུ་ཁག་པོ་མིན་ཀྱང་ད་ཆ་ང་ཚོས་གནས་ཚུལ་མང་པོ་ཞིག་ཤེས་རྟོག་ཐུབ་ཀྱི་ཡོད་པར་བརྟེན། ཡ་རབས་མཛངས་སྤྱོད་ལ་བརྒྱུད་འཛིན་བདག་སྐྱོང་ཡོད་མེད་དང་། རང་ཐོག་ལ་འགན་འཁྲི་གང་ཞིག་བབ་ཡོད་མེད། མི་རབས་རྗེས་མར་གང་འདྲ་ཞིག་བརྒྱུད་སྐྱོང་དགོས་མིན་བཅས་ལ་ང་ཚོས་སྣང་ཡང་བསམ་ཞིབ་བྱ་རྒྱུ་གལ་ཆེན་པོ་རེད། ད་ལྟའི་མི་རབས་འདི་འགྱུར་འགྲོས་ཀྱིས་མཚམས་ཤིག་ཡིན་པ་གསལ་པོ་རེད། འཛམ་གླིང་ཡོངས་སུ་ཕན་ཚུན་གོ་རྟོགས་སྤེལ་རེས་བྱེད་ཐུབ་ཀྱི་ཡོད་ཀྱང་། ཞི་བདེའི་ཆེད་དོན་ལྡན་གྱི་བགྲོ་གླེང་ལས་ཁ་གཏད་གདོང་གཏུགས་ཀྱི་ལངས་ཕྱོགས་དེ་མང་བ་ཡོང་བཞིན་པ་རེད།

འཛམ་གླིང་གི་ཆ་ཁ་ཤས་སུ་མིའི་རིགས་ལྟོགས་ཤི་ཐེབས་པ་དང་། སྲོག་ཆགས་གཞན་གྱི་རིགས་རྩ་སྟོངས་སུ་འགྲོ་བ་བཅས་ཀྱིས་མཚོན། དེང་དུས་ཀྱི་རྐྱེན་ངན་མང་པོ་འདི་དག་གིས་སྨད་དུ་བྱུང་བའི་ཚན་རིག་དང་འཕྲུལ་རིག་གི་དགེ་མཚན་བཟང་པོ་རྣམས་གལ་ཏེ་ཟིལ་གྱིས་མནན་མེད་ནའང་། ད་མཉམ་འགྲན་བཟོད་པ་ལྟ་བུར་གྱུར་ཡོད། ཕྱིའི་མཁའ་དབྱིངས་ལ་ཉམས་ཞིབ་མང་པོ་བྱེད་བཞིན་པ་དང་དུས……མཚུངས། ས་སྟེང་གི་རྒྱ་མཚོ་རྣམས་དང་། མཚོ་ཆེན་ཁག །ཆུ་གཙང་ཡོད་པའི་ས་ཁུལ་རྣམས་དུག་རྫས་ངན་པའི་ཀླབས་ཀྱིས་ཆེས་ཆེར་བསླད་ཅིང་། དེ་དག་ཏུ་གནས་འཚའ་བའི་སྲོག་ཆགས་རྣམས་ཀྱི་ཐད་ལ་ད་དུང་མི་ཤེས་པ་དང་གོ་ལོག་རྒྱ་ཆེར་བྱེད་བཞིན་ཡོད་པ་རེད།

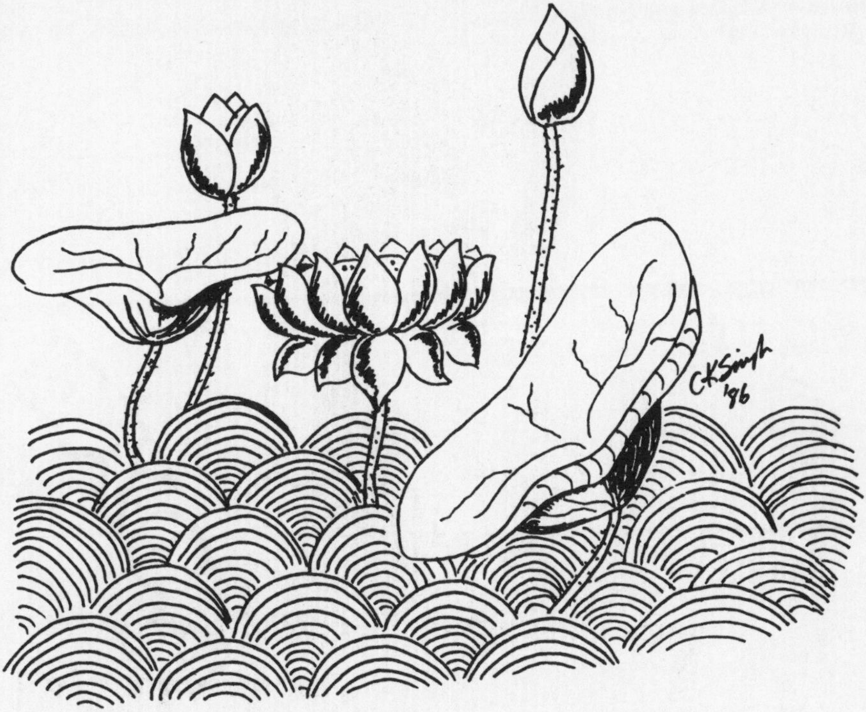

གླིང་འདིའི་སེམས་ཅན་གྱི་གནས་དང་། སེམས་ཅན་རྣམས་དང་། རྩི་ཤིང་རིགས་དང་། འབུ་སྲིན་རིགས་དང་། ཐ་ན་ཤིན་ཏུ་ཆེས་ཕྲ་བའི་སྲོག་ཆགས་རིགས་ད་ཆ་ང་ཚོས་དཀོན་པོར་ཤེས་པ་རྣམས་འབྱུང་འགྱུར་མི་རབས་རྣམས་ཀྱིས་གཏན་ནས་མི་ཤེས་པར་འགྱུར་ཉེན་ཡོད། དེའི་ཐད་ང་རང་ཚོར་ནུས་པ་དང་འགན་ཡོད། ང་རང་ཚོས་ཁྱེས་མ་དྭགས་གོང་ནས་ལག་ལེན་གྱི་བྱ་བ་ངེས་པར་བརྩམ་དགོས་པ་རེད།། །།

ཏཱ་ལའི་བླ་མས་ ༡༩༨༦ ཕྱི་ཟླ་༦ ཚེས་༥ ལ།

དབྱིན་ཡིག་ནས་བསྒྱུར་ཞུས།

༄༅། རང་བྱུང་ཁམས་སྲུང་སྐྱབ་སྐོར་ནང་ཆོས་ཀྱི་བསླབ་བྱ།

ཆཏ་ལུ་མན་ཀ་ཕྱིལ་སིང་།

ཕ་ཡི་ཡུལ་ལྷ་ཁང་ནི་ཐིང་ཁོག་གྲོང་འཁྱེར་ཉེ་འགྲམ་དུ་ཡོད་པའི་ནང་པའི་ལྷ་ཁང་ཞིག་རེད། ལྷ་ཁང་འདི་འགྱེལ་པ་མང་པོ་ཞིག་ལ་དགའ་བསུ་ཞུ་གི་ཡོད་པ་རེད། འགྱེལ་པ་དེ་རྣམས་བྱ་ཁྱུང་ཁྱུང་དཀར་མོའི་རིགས་ཤིག་རེད། བྱ་དེ་དག་སྟོན་ཁ་དང་དགུན་ཁ་ལྷ་ཁང་དེར་སྡོད་སྐབས་ལྷ་ཁང་དེ་དང་། ཤིང་སྡོང་ཚང་མ་བྱ་སྐྱག་གིས་དཀར་པོ་བཟོ་གི་ཡོད་པ་རེད། ཡིན་ནའང་ལྷ་ཁང་དེའི་དགེ་འདུན་པ་རྣམས་ཀྱི་དེར་ཐུགས་བསུན་མ་གནང་བ་དང་། བྱ་ལ་དགའ་བའི་སྐྱེ་བོ་རྣམས་ཀྱིས་དགའ་བསུའི་རང་བཞིན་དུ་འཆར་གྱི་ཡོད་པ་རེད། ཁྱུང་ཁྱུང་དཀར་མོའི་རིགས་འདི་བཞིན་ལྷ་ཁང་དེའི་ནང་གཞིས་ཆགས་རྒྱུ་བྱུང་ཐབ་པ་དེས་ས་གཏོགས་ཐ་ཡི་ལེན་ཉིར་བླ་རིགས་འདི་བཞིན་རྩ་སྟོང་འགྲོ་རྒྱུའི་ཉེན་ཁ་ཡོད་པ་རེད།

འཁོར་…ཡུག་དང་སྲོག་ཆགས་ཐོག་མཐུན་ལྡན་རྣམས་ཀྱི་བཞེད་ཚུལ་ལ་བྱ་རིགས་འདི་བཞིན་སྲུང་སྐྱབ་བྱེད་རྒྱུ་ནི་གལ་ཆེན་པོ་ཡིན་པ་རེད། གང་ལགས་ཟེར་ན་བྱ་འདིའི་ཟས་གཙོ་བོ་དེ་འབྲས་ཟ་མཁན་གྱི་སྨུག་པའི་འབུ་རིགས་ཞིག་ཡིན་པ་རེད། གལ་ཏེ་བྱ་དེ་མེད་པ་ཡིན་ན། འབུ་འདིའི་གྲངས་འཕེལ་རྒྱས་སུ་ཕྱིན་ནས་དེ་འགོག་ཐབས་སུ་འབུ་སྨན་བེད་སྤྱོད་བྱ་དགོས་བྱུང་ན་དེ་དུག་གི་ལས་ཀའི་འཁོར་ལོ་གསར་པ་ཞིག་འགོ་འཛུགས་རྒྱུ་ཡིན་པ་དེ་བརྗོད་མ་དགོས་པ་རེད།

ཁྱུང་ཁྱུང་གི་རིགས་འདི་སྐྱབ་པའི་ཞེ་པོ་གང་ཙམ་ནང་ཆོས་ཀྱི་བསླབ་བྱའི་ཐོག་ནས་སྤྱི་དང་སེར་གྱི་བྱ་སྤྱོད་ལ་བརྟེན་ནས་ཁྱུང་ཁྱུང་གི་རིགས་བསླབ་བྱས་འདི་བཞིན་སྲུང་སྐྱབ་བྱས་པའི་དངོས་དཔང་སྐྱབ་འབྲས་གསལ་པོ་ཞིག་རེད། ཉེ་བའི་ལོ་བཅུ་ཁྲག་འགའ་ཤས་རིང་ཟ་ཡི་རྒྱལ་ཁབ་ཀྱི་རང་བྱུང་ཁམས་ལ་གནོད་འཚེ་ཤུགས་ཆེར་བྱུང་ཡོད་པ་རེད། ལོ་ངོ་ལྔ་བཅུ་ཟིན་དུ་རྒྱལ་ཁབ་ཀྱི་ས་ཁྱོན་བརྒྱ་ཆ་ ༨༧ ཙམ་ནགས་ཚལ་གྱིས་ཁེངས་ནས་ཡོད་པ་ད་ཆ་བརྒྱ་ཆ་ ༡༣ ལས་མེད་པ་རེད། བྱ་བྱིའུ་དང་། རི་དྭགས་གཅན་གཟན། རྩི་ཤིང་སྔོ་ཚོགས་པ་མང་པོ་ཞིག་རྩ་སྟོང་འགྲོ་རྒྱུའི་ཉེན་ཁ་ཡོད་པ་མ་ཟད། རིགས་འགའ་ཤས་རྩ་མེད་དུ་ཕྱིན་ཟིན་པ་རེད།

ཟ་ཡི་ནང་རང་བྱུང་ཁམས་དང་རང་བྱུང་རྫས་ལ་ཉམས་ཆགས་ཆེན་པོ་ཕྱིན་ཡོད་པའི་རྐྱེན་གྱི་དེང་སང་གྲོང་གསེབ་ཁག་མང་པོའི་ནང་འཚོ་བའི་གནས་སྟངས་ཞན་པས་ཡུལ་མི་ཚོར་དཀའ་ངལ་མང་པོ་ཞིག་འཕྲད་ཀྱི་ཡོད་པ་རེད། རྒྱལ་ས་ཕིང་ཀོག་ལ་ཆུ་གློག་ཡང་སེ་ཡོང་གི་དཀའ་ངལ་དང་། ཡང་རྒྱལ་ཁབ་ཀྱི་བྱང་ཤར་ས་ཁུལ་ལ་ཆར་པ་དུས་ཐོག་མ་བབས་པའི་དཀའ་ངལ་སོགས་མདོར་ན་ཡུལ་མི་ཚོར་འཚོ་བ་བསྐྱལ་རྒྱུར་དཀའ་ངལ་ཧ་ཅང་ཡོད་པ་རེད།

ཟ་ཡི་ལེན་ཏ་ཡུལ་གྱི་རང་བྱུང་སྡོད་ལ་གནོད་སྐྱོན་ཤུགས་ཆེར་བྱུང་ཡོད་པ་རེད་ལ་དེང་སང་འཛམ་གླིང་ནང་རང་བྱུང་ཁམས་དང་། སྡོད་ལ་སྲུང་བརྩི་མེད་པའི་འདོད་རྫས་ཀྱིས་བེད་སྤྱོད་བྱེད་སྟངས་དེ་ལ་བལྟས་ཚོད་དུ་རང་བྱུང་ཁམས་དང་སྡོད་ཀྱི་རིགས་རྩ་མེད་འགྱུགས་མྱུར་འགྲོ་སྲིད་པ་རེད། དེ་འདྲར་བརྟེན་བྱ་ཁྱུང་ཁྱུང་གི་རིགས་དེ་དང་འདྲ་བའི་རང་བྱུང་ཁམས་དང་སྡོད་ཀྱི་རི་ཏ་མང་པོ་ཞིག་སེམས་ཅན་ཐམས་ཅད་ལ་ཕན་པའི་བསམ་བློ་གཏོང་དགོས་པའི་བསླབ་བྱ་དེའི་འབྲས་བུ་ཞིག་ཡིན་པ་རེད། ཡིནའང་རང་བྱུང་ཁམས་དང་། སྡོད་ཀྱི་གཏོར་གཞིགས་གཏོང་མཁན་ཀྱི་པོ་འདོད་རྫས་ཅན་དང་། ངོ་ཚ་མེད་མཁན་དེ་ཚོས་ཁོ་རེད་ཚོ་ཡིན་པའི་ཡིད་ཆེས་ཡོད་རེད། ནང་པ་ཅིས་བརྗོད་ཀྱི་མེད། ཇི་ལྟར་རང་བྱུང་ཁམས་དང་སྡོད་ཀྱི་ཐོག་ཆོས་ལུགས་འདྲ་མིན་དབར་ལྟ་སྤྱོད་འཁྱེར་ཕྱོགས་མི་འདྲ་བ་ཡོད་པ་བཞིན། དེའི་ཕོ་རོན་ལེན་ཕྱོགས་ཀྱང་མི་དང་། མིའི་དབར་ཁྱད་པར་ཆེན་པོ་ཡོད་པ་རེད། ཆོས་ལུགས་ཚང་མའི་ནང་མིའི་རྣམ་དཔྱོད་འདྲ་མིན་སྣ་ཚོགས་པ་བཞིན་འཛམ་གླིང་འདིའི་ནང་ནང་པ་མི་གྲངས་ས་ཡ་གསུམ་བརྒྱ་ནས་དྲུག་བརྒྱ་བར་ཡོད་པའི་ནང་ཁྱད་པར་འཕགས་པའི་སྐྱེས་བུ་དམ་པ་དང་། མིང་ཙམ་གྱི་ནང་པ་ཡིན་པ་སོགས་སྤྱིར་སྣ་ཚོགས་ཡོད་པ་རེད།

ནང་པ་སངས་རྒྱས་ཀྱི་ཆོས་ལུགས་ནི་སེར་གྱི་ལྟ་སྤྱོད་ལ་གལ་ཆེར་འཛིན་ཏེ་ལྟ་བ་དང་སྤྱོད་པ་གཉིས་ཐོག་ཞིབ་འཇུག་གི་ལམ་མ་ནོར་བར་ཉམས་ལེན་གྱི་ཐར་པ་ཐོབ་དགོས་པ་ཞིག་ཡིན་པ་རེད།

འཛམ་གླིང་གི་ཆོས་ལུགས་ཆེ་བ་གཞན་གྱི་ནང་དེ་འདྲ་བའི་བསླབ་བྱ་དང་། ངོས་འཛིན་བྱེད་སྲོལ་མེད་པ་དེས་ནང་པའི་ཆོས་ཀྱི་བསླབ་བྱ་ཕྱོང་མ་ཡིན་པ་ཞིག་ལ་ངོས་འཛིན་བྱེད་ཀྱི་ཡོད་པ་རེད།

རང་བྱུང་ཁམས་ཀྱི་ཚན་རིག་པས་རང་བྱུང་ཁམས་སྲུང་སྐྱོབ་དགོས་པའི་སློབ་གསོ་དང་། རྒྱུ་མཚན་མང་པོ་ཞིག་ནང་པ་སྒྱས་པའི་ཆོས་ཀྱི་བསླབ་བྱའི་ནང་ནས་ཐོབ་ཀྱི་ཡོད་པ་རེད།

ནང་ཆོས་ནང་རང་བྱུང་ཁམས་དབང་དུ་འགྱུར་བ་ལས་མཉམ་དུ་གནས་ཐབས་པ་དེ་གལ་ཆེ་ཡིན་པ་བསླབས་ཡོད་པ་རེད། ནང་ཆོས་གཏིང་ཟབ་ཉམས་ལེན་གནང་མཁན་རྣམས་ཀྱི་ངོ་ ཚོ་ཁྲིལ་མེད་ཀྱི་གནོད་འཚེའི་བྱ་སྤྱོད་མ་རུང་བར་བྱེད་པ་ལས་རང་བྱུང་ཁམས་སྲུང་སྐྱོབ་ཡོང་རྒྱུར་སྟྭ་ཞེན་གནང་གི་ཡོད་པ་རེད།

ནང་ཆོས་ཀྱི་སྙིང་དོན་ནི་སྙིང་རྗེ་ཡིན་པ་རེད། དེ་བཞིན་འཛམ་གླིང་འདིའི་ཐང་གི་འགྲོ་བ་མི་དང་ཕྱུགས་ཆགས་གཞན་རྣམས་ལ་བརྩེ་མཐོངས་ཐང་བཟོད་སེམས་ཀྱི་མཉམ་དུ་གནས་དགོས་པའི་བསྒྲགས་གཙོན་སྟོན་གྱི་ཡོད་པ་རེད། ང་ཚོས་བརྟག་ཞིབ་བྱས་པའི་སྙིང་པོར་ནང་ཆོས་ཉམས་ལེན་བྱེད་མཁན་གྱི་ཡུལ་མང་པོའི་ནང་རང་བྱུང་ཁམས་ལ་སྲུང་སྐྱོབ་བྱེད་རྒྱུར་ཕན་ཡོན་ཆེན་པོ་བྱུང་ཡོད་པ་རེད། དཔེར་ན། ལང་གའི་ཡུལ་གྱི་རི་དྭགས་མང་ཆེ་བ་ཐར་རྒྱུན་བཞིན་གནས་ཐུབ་ཡོད་པ་དེ་ནི་ཡུལ་མི་རྣམས་དང་ཀུན་ནང་པ་ཡིན་པའི་རྐྱེན་གྱི་རེད། ཅེས་ཉམས་ཞིབ་བྱེད་མཁན་ཆོས་བཤད་ཀྱི་ཡོད།

རང་བྱུང་ཁམས་སྲུང་སྐྱོབ་བྱེད་རྒྱུ་དེ་ནི་གཞུང་འབྲེལ་གྱི་ལས་འགུལ་འགོ་འཛུགས་བྱས་པ་ཞིག་ཡིན། དེ་ནི་ཡུལ་དེའི་མི་མང་ནས་ཁས་ལེན་དང་། འདོད་སྤྲོ་མེད་ཚེ་གྲུབ་འབྲས་ཐོན་རྒྱུར་ཕན་ནུས་དེ་ཙམ་མེད་པ་རེད། རང་བྱུང་ཁམས་རྒྱུན་གནས་ཐུབ་པའི་ལས་འགུལ་གྱི་གྲུབ་འབྲས་ལེགས་པོ་བྱུང་བ་དེ་དག་གཙོ་བོ་ནང་དོན་རིག་པའི་བསམ་བློ་འཁྱེར་ཕྱོགས་ལ་རག་ལུས་ཡོད་པ་རེད།

ང་ཚོའི་བོད་རིགས་ཉམས་ཞིབ་འགན་འཛིན་རྣམས་ཀྱིས་ཉེ་བའི་འཆར་ལོ་རྒྱས་དུན་ཐོག་ལ་བོད་ནང་རྐ་བ་དང་། གཡག འབྲོང་། ཤ་བ། དེ་བཞིན་བྱ་རིགས་ཀྱི་ཁྱུ་ལ་སོགས་པ་མང་པོ་ཞིག་མིའི་རྫོད་གནས་འཁྱག་ས་སྐུར་འཇིགས་སྣང་མེད་པའི་ངང་ཡོང་ནས་མཉམ་དུ་བརྡད་པ་སྐྱ་ཡོང་གི་ཡོད་པ་རེད། དེ་ནི་བོད་དེ་བཞིན་ནང་པའི་རྒྱལ་ཁབ་གཅིག་ཡིན་པའི་རྒྱུ་མཚན་ལ་བརྟེན་ནས་བྱུང་བ་ཞིག་རེད།

ཕྱ་ཁས་པའི་གནས་ཚུལ་ཞིག་ལ་གནས.ཏ་ངས་དེ་འགྱུར་བ་ཕྱིན་ནས་ད་ཆ་བོད་ནི་རང་བྱུང་ཁམས་དང་ཕྱུགས་ཆགས་སོགས་ལ་རྗོད་འཚེ་ཇེ་མང་བྱུང་བའི་ཡུལ་ཞིག་ཏུ་བཅོས་ཀྱི་ཡོད་པ་རེད།

འཛམ་གླིང་མཉམ་འབྲེལ་རྒྱལ་ཚོགས་ཀྱི་འགྲོ་བ་མིའི་ཐོབ་འཐང་གི་ཚོགས་ཆུང་ལ་ཕུལ་བའི་དམིགས་བསལ་ལས་བརྩམས་དེའི་ནང་། བོད་ཀྱི་རྩི་ཤིང་ནགས་ཚལ་གྱིས་ཁྱབ་པའི་ས་ཆ་རྒྱ་ཆེ་རྩ་མེད་བཟོས་པ་དང་སྔར་རི་དྭགས་མང་པོ་གནས་པ་དེ་དག་ད་ཆ་རྩ་མེད་དུ་བཏང་ཡོད་པ་རེད་ཅེས་བཀོད་ཡོད་པ་རེད།

སངས་རྒྱས་ཀྱི་བསྟན་པའི་ལོ་རྒྱུས་ནང་ནང་ཆོས་ཀྱིས་རང་བྱུང་ཁམས་སྲུང་སྐྱོབ་ཐོག་ཕན་ཆེན་པོ་བྱས་ཡོད་པ་རེད། ཉེ་བའི་འཆར་ནང་པའི་འགོ་འཁྲིད་ཆོས་གནས་དོན་འདྲའི་ཐོག་ནང་ཆོས་ལས་བཤད་པའི་ནང་དོན་རིག་པའི་བསླབ་བྱ་རྣམས་རང་བྱུང་ཁམས་སྲུང་སྐྱོབ་དང་སྔར་ཡོད་རྒྱུན་གནས་ཡོང་ཐབས་སུ་ཕན་ཐོགས་དང་། ཞབས་འདེགས་ཞུ་ཐུབ་ཀྱི་ཡོད་པའི་གསུང་གླེང་གནང་གི་ཡོད་པ་རེད།

༧གོང་ས་༧སྐྱབས་མགོན་ཏཱ་ལའི་བླ་མ་མཆོག་ནས་གསར་འགོད་པར་བཀའ་བཙལ་གསལ། དེང་སང་སྔར་ལས་ལྷག་པར་ང་ཚོས་རྒྱལ་སྤྱིའི་ལས་འགན་ཐོག་སེམས་འཁུར་བྱེད་དགོས་པ་ཞིག་ཡིན་ལ། དེ་ཡང་རྒྱལ་ཁབ་ཕན་ཚུན་དང་། མི་དང་མིའི་བར་དུ་མ་ཟད། མི་དང་སྲོག་ཆགས་གཞན་གྱི་རི་ཀ་ལའང་སེམས་འཁུར་བྱེད་དགོས་པ་ཡིན།

སྤྱི་ཚོགས་ཀྱི་གནས་སྟངས་ཉམས་ཞིབ་པ་དང་རྩོམ་པ་པོ་སུ་ལག་ ཤི་བ་རག་སས་གསུངས་གསལ་འཛམ་གླིང་འདི་བཞིན་རྙོག་འཛིངས་གང་འདྲ་ཞིག་ཏུ་འགྱུར་བ་ཡིན་ནའང་། ནང་ཆོས་ཀྱི་བསླབ་བྱ་དེ་དག་ཁ་ཡོད་ལག་ཡོད་ཕན་ནུས་ཡོད་པ་དང་སྤྱི་ཚོགས་ཀྱི་ཡར་རྒྱས་དང་། མཐུན་བསྒྲིལ་ཡོང་རྒྱུར་ཕན་ནུས་ཐུབ་པའི་གལ་ཆེའི་གཞི་རྩ་ཞིག་ཆགས་ཡོད་པ་རེད། ཀུ་ཞབས་སུ་ལག་ ཤི་བ་རག་ས་ཁོ་རང་ལ་གླིང་ཆེན་ཨེ་ཤ་ཡ་དང་འཛམ་གླིང་འཕོ་འགྱུར་འགྲོ་བའི་ནང་ཐ་ཡི་ནང་པའི་ཆོས་ཀྱི་སྐད་འབོད་ཅེས་དང་། ཆེད་བརྗོད་ཀྱི་མིང་འབོད་བྱེད་ཀྱི་ཡོད་པ་རེད།

བོད་རང་རང་བྱུང་ཁམས་ལ་གནོད་སྐྱོན་ཡོང་གི་ཡོད་པར་བརྟེན་བོད་རང་གིས་ནང་ཆོས་ཐོག་ནས་དེ་དག་སྲུང་སྐྱོབ་བྱེད་ཐུབ་པའི་ཡིད་མཆེས་ཀྱིས་ཐོག་ནང་ཆོས་ཀྱིས་རང་བྱུང་ཁམས་སྲུང་སྐྱོབ་བྱེད་དགོས་པའི་རྩོམ་ཡིག་དང་སྔོན་དུ་པར་དང་ཀྲ་རྡུང་ཀླུབ་ཐག་ཐོག་གསུང་བཤད་གནང་བ་སོགས་ཀྱི་སློབ་སྟོན་གནང་གི་ཡོད་པ་རེད།

ད་དུང་མི་རྣམས་ཀྱི་དོ་གལ་ཆེ་ཆུང་ལ་མ་ལྟོས་པར་རང་བྱུང་ཁམས་ལ་གནོད་འཚེ་བྱེད་བཞིན་པ་དེའི་ཐོག་ནང་ཆོས་ཀྱིས་དེར་ང་རྒོལ་བྱེད་ཀྱི་ཡོད་པ་རེད། ང་རྒོལ་དེ་ད་ལྟ་ཆུང་ཆུང་ཞིག་ཡིན་ནའང་། ཞི་བའི་ཐོག་ནས་ལས་འགུལ་བྱས་པ་འདི་མེད་པ་ལས་དྭག་པ་ཞིག་ཡིན་པ་དང་།

གལ་ཏེ་བསླབ་བྱ་དེ་དག་གལ་ཆེར་རྩིས་ནས་ལག་ལེན་དུ་བཀལ་ན་རང་བྱུང་ཁམས་ཟེར་ཡོད་རྒྱུན་གནས་ཐུབ་ཐབས་ལ་ལས་འགུལ་དེ་བཞིན་ང་ཚོའི་ལུང་པའི་ནང་ཤུགས་ཆེ་རུ་འགྲོ་རྒྱུ་རེད་ཅེས་གསུངས་ཡོད་པ་རེད།

ཉི་ཧོང་སྲིད་འཛིན་ཡ་སུ་ཧི་རོ་ ན་ཀ་སོ་ནེ་མཆོག་ནས་ཕྱི་ལོ་ ༡༩༨༥ ལོར་མཉམ་སྦྲེལ་རྒྱལ་ཚོགས་ཀྱི་ཁྲ་བྱུ་བསྐྱེས་པའི་དུས་དྲན་མཛད་རིགས་བཅས་ནས་འཛམ་གླིང་འདིའི་རང་བཞིན་འཛོམས་རྡུག་དང་། རིག་འདྲ་མིན་སྣ་ཚོགས་ཡོད་པ་སུ་མཐུད་གནས་ཐུབ་ཐབས་ཀྱི་འབོད་བསྐུལ་ཞུས་གནང་ཡོད་པ་རེད།

སླར་ཡང་ནང་ཆོས་ཀྱི་ཐོག་ནས་གསུང་བཤད་གནང་བ་དེའི་འབོད་བསྐུལ་དུ་འཛམ་གླིང་གི་ཀུན་སྤྱོད་གསར་པ་དགོས་རྒྱུ་ཞེས་པ་དེ་ནི་དུས་རབས་ཉི་ཤུ་པ་འདི་བཞིན་མི་རིགས་བར་ཚུན་ལ་བརྩེ་བཀུར་དང་། མཉམ་གནས་ཐུབ་པ་དང་། མི་དང་རང་བྱུང་ཁམས་དབར་འབྲེལ་འཚམས་ཆ་སྙོམས་ཡོང་བའི་དུས་ཀབས་ཞེས་བརྗོད་ཐུབ་པ་བྱེད་རྒྱུ་དེ་ཡིན།

ཆེས་ཟ་མོའི་དུས་ཀྱི་ནང་ཆོས་ཀྱི་བསླབ་བྱ་རྣམས་དུས་དེང་སང་གི་དགོས་དོན་ཐོག་ཕན་ཐོགས་ཡོད་པར་ངེས་འཛིན་བྱེད་མཁན་ཇི་མང་འགྲོ་བཞིན་པ་རེད།

ཐ་ཡི་མཁས་པ་ཕི་ཡ་ཧ་སི་གསུངས་གསལ་ལ་དེའི་རྒྱུ་མཚན་གཅིག་ནི། སྟོན་པ་བཅོམ་ལྡན་འདས་ཁོང་གི་བཀའ་དང་གསུངས་ཆོས་རྣམས་ཤེས་བྱ་ཙམ་དུ་མ་ཡིན་པར་དོན་དངོས་ལག་ལེན་དུ་འཁྱོལ་དགོས་པ་དེ་གལ་ཆེ་ཡིན་གསུང་པ་དེ་རེད་ཅེས་བརྗོད་ཡོད།

དབྱིན་ཇིའི་རྩོམ་པ་པོ་མེཀ་ཇི་ཐེལ་སི་ ནས་ནང་ཆོས་ཐོག་སློབ་སྦྱོང་གནང་ནས་མཐར་མ་གསུངས་གསལ། སྟོན་པའི་གསུངས་རྣམས་གསལ་པོ་དང་། དེང་དུས་ཀྱི་རིག་པ་དང་། བསམ་བློ་གཏོང་ཕྱོགས་སོགས་དང་མཐུན་པོ་ཡོད་པ་དང་། འཛམ་གླིང་འདིའི་ཤང་ནང་དོན་རིག་པ་གཏིང་ཟབ་པོས་ཡིན་པར་ངེས་འཛིན་བྱས་པར་རྩོད་པ་མེད་པ་ཞིག་རེད།

དཔེར་ན། ནང་ཆོས་ཀྱི་ཐོག་ནས་རང་བྱུང་ཁམས་ལ་བརྟག་ངས་ཀྱི་ལས་འགུལ་དང་། འདྲ་བ་ཤེས་ཡོན་གྱི་ལས་རིགས་གཞན་ལ་ནང་ཆོས་ཀྱི་དམིགས་བསལ་ཤེས་བྱ་གསར་པའི་རིགས་བྲད་ཐུབ་ཀྱི་ཡོད་པ་རེད། མ་རིགས་པ་ཤེས་རབ་ཀྱི་གསལ་ཡག་ཡིན་ཙན་ནང་ཆོས་ཉམས་ཞིབ་བྱེད་མཁན་ཀྱི་ཕོ་

ས་འདྲ་ཞིག་ཡིན་རུང་མ་རིགས་པ་དོར་ཏེ་ཤེས་རབ་དང་ཤེས་བྱ་ཧྲོན་དགོས་པ་ཞིག་རེད། དེ་བཞིན་དགེ་བའི་བཤེས་གཉེན་ལ་བཙིགས་བཀུར་དང་། ནང་པའི་སློབ་དཔོན་ཁྱད་པར་དུ་འཕགས་པ་རྣམས་ལ་བསྙེན་བཀུར་བྱེད་དགོས་པ་ཡིན། དགེ་རྒན་ཚོས་རང་གི་སློབ་མ་རྣམས་རང་བྱུང་ཁམས་སྲུང་སྐྱོབ་ལས་འགུལ་ཉམས་ལེན་ཡོང་བའི་སློབ་གསོ་གནང་རྒྱུའི་མཐུན་རྐྱེན་ཆེད་དུ་ཡིག་ཆ་སོགས་པའི་ལག་ཆ་དགོས་ཀྱི་རེད། ང་ཚོའི་ལས་འགུལ་ཉམས་ཞིབ་པ་རྣམས་ནས་ལོ་ངོ་ ༡༥༠༠ ལྷག་ཙམ་སྔོན་གི་རྒྱ་ཆེ་ལ་གཏིང་ཟབ་པའི་ནང་ཆོས་ཀྱི་གསུང་རབ་རྣམས་ཀྱང་རིགས་འདྲ་མིན་ནང་ཡོད་པ་བཅས་ལ་ཉམས་ཞིབ་གནང་སྟེ་མཐུན་རྐྱེན་སྤྲོད་ཐུབ་དགོས་པའི་ལས་འགན་ཡོད་པ་རེད། དོན་འགྲོའི་ཉམས་ཞིབ་ལས་འགུལ་བྱས་རྗེས་ཡིག་ཆ་རྣམས་ཁག་གཅིག་ཏུ་བསྡུ་རྒྱུ་རེད། དེའང་དུད་འགྲོ་དང་། རྩི་ཤིང་ནགས་ཚལ་ཆུའི་ཐོན་ཁུངས་སོགས་མདོར་ན། རང་བྱུང་ཁམས་ཡོངས་རྫོགས་འགྲོ་བ་མིར་དགོས་མཁོ་ཡོད་ལ་ལས་འགན་ཀྱང་ཡོད་པའི་སྐོར་ནང་ཆོས་ཀྱི་གཞུང་ནས་གསུངས་པའི་བསླབ་བྱ་རྣམས་ཕྱོགས་བསྒྲིགས་བྱས་ནས་འགྲེམས་སྤེལ་བྱ་རྒྱུ་ཡིན་པ་ཕར་བྱུང་མ་སོང་བ་ཞིག་རེད།

ནང་ཆོས་ཀྱི་ནགས་ཚལ་སྟུག་པོ་དང་། དབེན་གནས་སུ་གནས་པའི་སྒོམ་ཆེན་སོགས་ལ་གལ་ཆེ་རྩིས་པ་དང་། དེ་བཞིན་རི་དྭགས་དང་རྩི་ཤིང་སོགས་མང་པོ་སྲོག་ཆགས་ཀྱི་རིགས་རྣམས་དཔེ་རྒྱན་ཇི་འདྲ་ཞིག་ཆོས་རྫས་ཀྱིས་མཚོན་བྱེད་དུ་འཛིན་པ་རྣམས་ལ་རང་བྱུང་ཁམས་སྲུང་སྐྱོབ་བྱེད་རྒྱུའི་བསླབ་བྱའི་ཡིག་ཆ་རྒྱ་ཆེ་འཚོལ་སྒྲུབ་བྱེད་ཐུབ་པ་དེར་ཡ་མཚན་གྱིས་དགོས་པའི་རྒྱུ་མཚན་གང་ཡང་མེད་པ་ཞིག་རེད།

རབ་བྱུང་རྣམས་ཤིང་གཅོད་མི་ཆོག་པ་རེད། དེ་ཡང་ཚང་མས་ཤེས་གསལ་ལྟར་སྔོན་གྲྭ་པ་ཞིག་གིས་ཤིང་སྡོང་གི་ཡལ་ག་ཞིག་བཅད་པའི་རྗེས་སུ་ཤིང་དེར་གནས་པའི་ལྷ་དེས་ཁོ་རང་གི་བུའི་ལག་པ་ཡ་གཅིག་བཅད་སོང་ཞེས་བཅོམ་ལྡན་འདས་ལ་དེ་ཞུས་པའི་ལོ་རྒྱུས་ཡོད་པ་རེད།

ཡང་ལོ་རྒྱུས་ཀྱི་བསླབ་བྱ་གཞན་ཞིག་ལ་ཕར་འགྲུལ་པ་འགའ་ཞིག་བྱང་ཆུབ་སྡོང་ཤིང་དེས་གྲོགས་པོ་ཕར་འགྲུལ་པ་རྣམས་ལ་ཉི་མ་ཚ་བའི་སྐབས་གྲིབ་གསིལ་སྤྲོད་པའི་ཕན་འབྲས་དེར་གྲོགས་པོ་དེར་གནོད་པ་བྱས་པའི་བྱ་སྤྱོད་ངན་པ་དེར་ཀུན་འཛུགས་བྱས་ཡོད་པ་རེད།

ཨན་གུ་ཏ་ར་ ནི་ཀ་ཡའི་ཕྱག་དཔེའི་ནང་། དེ་དང་འདྲ་བའི་ལོ་རྒྱུས་ཞིག་ཡོད་པ་རེད། ཕར་ར་ཛ་ཀོ་རན་ཡ་ཞེས་པ་ཞིག་ལ་བྱང་ཆུབ་སྡོང་ཆེན་པོ་ཞིག་ཡོད་པ་དེའི་མིང་ལ་བརྟན་པོ་ཞེས་ཟེར་ཞིང་། ཤིང་དེའི་ཡལ་ག་རྒྱ་ཆེ་ལ་རིང་ཚད་དཔག་ཚད་བཅུ་གཅིག་ཙམ་ཡོད་པའི་གྲིབ་གསིལ་ཅན་

པ་ཞིག་ཡོད། ཤིང་དེའི་འབྲས་བུ་རྣམས་ལ་སྲུང་བུ་བྱེད་དགོས་པ་མ་ཟད། འབྲས་བུ་ཟིན་རྗེས་ཤིང་དེར་གནོད་སྐྱོན་གཏོང་མཁན་སུ་ཡང་ཡོད་པ་མ་རེད། ཉིན་གཅིག་ཨེ་ཞིག་ཡོང་ནས་ཤིང་དེའི་འབྲས་བུ་རྒྱག་ཚོད་ཟིན་རྗེས་ཡལ་ག་གཅིག་ཀྱང་བཅག་ནས་བྱིན་པ་རེད། ཤིང་དེར་གནས་པའི་ལྷ་དེའི་བསམ་ཚུལ་ལ། རང་གི་འདོད་པ་འཁེངས་པའི་འབྲས་བུ་ཟིན་རྗེས་ཤིང་དེའི་ཡལ་ག་ཡང་བཅག་པ་དེ་འདྲའི་མི་ངན་པ་ལ་ཀ་བསམས་པ་རེད། གལ་སྲིད་ཤིང་སྡོང་དེར་འབྲས་བུ་མ་སྐྱིས་པ་ཡིན་ན་བསམས་ཀ་བས་རྗེས་སུ་ཤིང་དེར་འབྲས་བུ་ཙ་བ་ནས་སྐྱིས་མེད་པ་རེད།

དེ་འདྲ་བའི་ནང་ཆོས་ཀྱི་བསླབ་བྱའི་ཐོག་ནས་གྲྭ་པ་དང་། སྐྱེ་བོ་རྣམས་ལ་ཅི་ཤིང་གི་རིགས་དེ་དག་མི་ཙམ་མ་ཡིན་པར་ནགས་གཞིབ་ཏུ་གནས་པའི་རི་དྭགས་སོགས་ལའང་ཟས་དང་། བསིལ་གྲིབ་དང་སྲུང་སྐྱབ་སོགས་ཀྱི་ཕན་ཐོགས་ཡོད་པར་བརྟེན་དེ་ཚོར་གནོད་འཚེ་བྱེད་རྒྱུ་མེད་པའི་ལམ་སྟོན་སྤྲད་ཀྱི་ཡོད་པ་རེད།

ནགས་ཚལ་ལ་ཅིས་མཐོང་ས་བྱུས་པར་ནགས་ཚལ་རྒྱ་ཆེན་པོ་ཙ་མེད་བཟོས་པའི་རྐྱེན་གྱི་དེང་སང་ས་རུལ་རྒྱབ་པ་དང་ཆུ་རག་མེད་པའི་རྐྱེན་གྱི་མཐའ་མ་ས་ལ་ཞིང་ལ་ཁོན་འབྲས་ལ་ཤིན་པ་དང་། སྲོག་ཆགས་དང་རྩི་ཤིང་རིགས་རྣམས་ཀྱང་གནས་ཡུལ་མེད་པའི་རྐྱེན་གྱི་ཙ་ཁོང་དུ་འགྲོ་གི་ཡོད་པ་རེད།

ལོ་ ༡༥༠༠ ཙམ་སྔོན་དང་། རང་བྱུང་ཁམས་དབར་མཉམ་གནས་ཀྱི་སྐྱི་ཚོགས་ཞིག་ནང་ནང་པ་སངས་རྒྱས་པའི་ཆོས་དེ་ཙ་བ་ཚུགས་པ་ཞིག་ཡིན་ནའང་། འཛམ་གླིང་འདིའི་རང་བྱུང་ཁམས་ཐོག་ཉམས་སྐྱོད་ངན་པ་བྱུས་ན་དེའི་འབྲས་བུ་ཇི་འདྲ་ཡོང་མིན་དུས་སྐབས་དེ་ནས་གསལ་པོ་ཤེས་ཀྱི་ཡོད་པ་རེད། དཔེར་ན་བྲམ་ཟེའི་ལོ་རྒྱུས་ཞིག་ནང་། བྲམ་ཟེ་དེས་སྟོན་པ་བཅོམ་ལྡན་འདས་ལ་མི་འཕར་ཉུང་དུ་འགྲོ་བའི་རྒྱུ་མཚན་ཇི་ཡིན་བཀའ་དྲི་ཞུས་སྐབས། སྟོན་པས་གསུངས་གསལ། མི་རྣམས་ཁྲིམས་མེད་འདོད་ཆགས་ཀྱི་མི་རྩི་འཕར་བ་དང་། མ་རུང་བའི་རེ་འདུན་གྱིས་འཁྱིངས་ཤིང་།། ལྟ་བུ་ཐོག་པར་རྗེས་འདུངས་ཀྱིས་རྫོངས་སུ་བཅུག་པའི་རྐྱེན་གྱི་གནམ་ནས་ཆར་པ་དུས་ཐོག་མ་བཏང་བ་དང་། ལོ་ཏོག་རྒྱ་ཡང་ཁག་པོ་ཡོད་པ་དང་ལོ་ཏོགས་ཞན་ལ། ནད་ཐོགས་པ་སོགས་ རྫ་ཙམ་ལས་ཀྱིས་མི་ཐུབ་པར་བརྟེན་མི་གྲངས་ཉུང་དུ་འགྲོ་གི་ཡོད་པ་རེད།

ནང་ཆོས་ཀྱི་གཞུང་ནང་སྲོག་བཅད་པའམ་གཅོད་རྒྱུའི་ཀུན་སློང་འཁྱེར་བ་ཙམ་གྱི་མི་དགེ་བའི་ལས་བསགས་ཀྱི་ཡོད་པར་བརྟེན་ནང་ཆོས་ཉམས་ལེན་གཏིང་ཟབ་གནང་མཁན་ཚོས་ཤིང་ཏོག་དང་།

ཚལ། འབྲུ་སོགས་ལ་འཚོ་བའི་ཡོ་བྱད་ཡོངས་སུ་ཕྱུད་ནས་ལུད་རྟགས་ཉམས་ཞེན་གནང་གི་ཡོད་པ་རེད། དེ་རྐྱ་བུའི་འབྲས་བུས་རྫོན་ཤིང་དང་། འབུ་སོགས་ལ་གནོད་འཚེ་བྱེད་རྒྱུ་མེད་པ་ཞིག་རེད།

ནང་ཆོས་ཀྱི་གཞུང་ནས་འཇིག་རྟེན་འདིའི་སྟེང་འགྲོ་བ་ཟིའི་རིགས་ནི་དམིགས་བསལ་གྱི་གལ་གནད་ཡིན་པ་ཞིག་ཅིས་ཀྱི་ཡོད་པ་རེད། དེ་ནི་འགྲོ་བ་མིར་རྣམ་དཔྱོད་ཀྱི་ཐོག་ནས་ཐག་གཅོད་བྱེད་རྒྱུ་ཡོད་པ་དེ་ཡིན།

འཛམ་གླིང་གི་ས་ཕྱོགས་འགར་གང་ཟག་འགའ་ཞིག་ཚལ་རིགས་རྐྱང་པའི་ཟས་ཀྱིས་ལུས་སྟོབས་ཉམས་པས་རྐྱེན་གྱི་སེམས་ཀྱི་ནུས་པ་དང་ཡར་རྒྱས་འགྲོ་རྒྱུར་གནོད་ཀྱི་ཡོད་པ་རེད། དེ་འདྲར་བརྟེན་ནང་ཆོས་ཀྱི་ཐོག་ནས་ཟས་ཟ་ཚོག་མི་ཚོག་གེར་སོགས་བཅའ་ཁྲིམས་བྱས་ཤིང་། གསལ་བ་ཡོད་པ་དེ་དག་ཞིབ་འཇུག་ཚི་ཚན་ནས་བརྟག་ཞིབ་བྱེད་བཞིན་རེད། དཔེར་འདི་འདྲ་བའི་ཟོ་སྤྱོད་ཅོམ་བསྒྲིགས་ཁག་གི་ནང་དོན་སྙིང་པོ་ནི། འགྲོ་བ་མིའི་བྱ་སྤྱོད་མཐའ་དག་རང་བྱུང་འཁོར་ཡུག་ལ་སྲུང་བརྩི་དགོས་པ་ལས་རང་འདོད་ཀྱིས་རྩ་མེད་བཟོ་མི་རུང་བའི་བསླབ་བྱ་བསྟན་གྱི་ཡོད་པ་རེད།

ནང་ཆོས་ཐོག་ནས་སྲོག་ཆགས་ཚང་མ་ཉིན་གཅིག་ཐར་པའི་ལམ་དུ་འགྲོ་རྒྱུའི་གོ་སྐབས་ཡོད་པ་ཞིག་ལ་ངོས་འཛིན་བྱེད་ཀྱི་ཡོད་པ་རེད། འགྲོ་བ་མི་རྣམས་མཐོ་རིས་ཀྱི་གྲས་སུ་ཡོད་ནའང་རང་བྱུང་ཁམས་དང་། སྲོག་ཆགས་སོགས་ལ་དབང་བསྒྱུར་བྱས་པར་འགྲོ་བ་མིའི་རིགས་རྣམས་ཉེན་ཁའི་ནང་ལྷུང་བའི་བྱ་སྤྱོད་ཞིག་ཡིན་པར་ངོས་འཛིན་བྱེད་ཀྱི་ཡོད་པ་རེད། ནང་ཆོས་ཐོག་ནས་རང་བྱུང་ཁམས་ལ་རྩ་ཕྱོགས་ཕོད་པའི་ཉམས་ཞིབ་པ་ཀུ་ཤ་བས་ཀ་ཚ་དགེ་ལེགས་གཡུ་ཐོག་ནས་ཐེག་པ་ཆེན་པོའི་གཞུང་ནས་སེམས་ཅན་ཐམས་ཅད་ལ་བྱམས་སྙིང་རྗེ་དགོས་པའི་སྐོར་སྦྱུག་རྒྱུར་བཀོན་ཞུས་པ་གཤམ་གསལ།

སྟོན་པའི་ཆོས་དེ་རྩ་བ་སྙིང་རྗེ་ཡིན། དེ་ལ་སྐྱབས་བཅོལ་གང་ཟག་སུ་ཞིག་གིས།
སེམས་ཅན་གཞན་ལ་སྙིང་རྗེའི་བསླབ་ཇོམ་གྱིས། གནོད་འཚེའི་ལས་ཀྱི་བྱ་བ་བྱེད་མི་རུང་།

དེ་བཞིན་སེམས་ཅན་གཞན་ལ་གནོད་འཚེ་བྱེད་རྒྱུ་ཐོངས་དགོས་པའི་སྐོར་རྗེ་ཙོང་ཁ་པ་ཆེན་པོས།

སེམས་ཅན་ལ་གནོད་འཚེ་བྱ་རྒྱུའི་བསམ་སྤྱོད་གཉིས་ཀའི་ཐོག་ནས་ཐོངས་དགོས་པ་ཞིག་ཡིན། དེ་ཡང་མི་དང་དུད་འགྲོ་སོགས་བརྡུང་བ་དང་། ཐག་པས་བཅམས་པ་དང་། བཙོན་དུ་བཙུག་པ། ཟ་ཁུག་ཏུ་ཤིག་གསང་བཀོན་པ། སེམས་ཅན་དེའི་ལུས་སྟོབས་ཀྱིས་ནུས་ཤུགས་ལས་རྒྱག་པའི་ཁལ་ཆེན་པོ་བཀུར་བའི་སྤྱོད་པ་ལ་སོགས་བྱེད་མི་རུང་ཞེས་གསུངས།

དེ་བཞིན་རྫོགས་ཆེན་དཔལ་སྤྲུལ་འཇིགས་མེད་དབང་པོའི་ཀུན་བཟང་བླ་མའི་ཞལ་ལུང་ནང་། ཆོས་ལ་སྐྱབས་བཅོལ་བའི་རྗེས་སུ་སེམས་ཅན་གཞན་ལ་གནོད་འཚེ་སྤོང་དགོས་པ་ཡིན། དེ་ཡང་གནོད་འཚེའི་ལས་ཀ་ནི་རང་གི་མི་ལམ་དུ་འཁོར་མི་རུང་བར་བརྟེན། ལས་དེ་རིགས་སྤོང་ཐབས་སུ་འབད་བརྩོན་བྱེད་དགོས་ཞེས་གསུང་ཡོད། སེམས་ཅན་གཞན་ལ་གནོད་འཚེ་སྤོངས་རྒྱུ་དེ་ནི་ནང་པའི་སྐྱེས་བུ་དམ་པ་རྣམས་ཀྱིས་བྱམས་པ་དང་། སྙིང་རྗེ། གཞན་ཕན་སོགས་ཀྱི་སྤྱོད་སོགས་ལ་བརྟེན་པའི་ཐོག་མ་དེ་ཡིན། སྟོན་པ་བཅོམ་ལྡན་འདས་ཀྱིས་བྱམས་བརྩེ་དེ་གལ་ཆེ་ཡིན་པའི་སྐོར་གསུངས་ཡོད།

འཛམ་གླིང་བྱེ་བ་མང་པོའི་རྒྱ་ནོར་ཕུན་སུམ་ཚོགས་ལ་རྒྱ་ཆེ་བའི་མཆོད་པ་དུས་རྟག་ཏུ་དཀོན་མཆོག་གསུམ་ལ་ཕུལ་བ་དེ་སྐད་ཅིག་ཙམ་གྱི་བྱམས་སྙིང་རྗེ་བྱས། དེའི་ཕན་ཡོན་དང་འགྲན་མི་ཐུབ། ཡང་ནང་པའི་ཆོས་ཀྱི་གཙོ་བོ་སྙིང་རྗེ་ཡིན་པ་དཔེ་མཚོན་གཞན་ཞིག་ནས་བརྗོད་ན། ཤ་མས་རང་གི་སྡུག་ལ་ཐུག་ཀྱང་། སོ་སོའི་བུ་གུ་སྐྱོང་སྐྱོབ་བྱེད་ཀྱི་ཡོད་པ་བཞིན་ཚང་མས་གཞན་གྱི་སྡུག་ཀྱང་སོ་སོའི་སྡུག་དང་མཚུངས་པའི་བསམ་བློ་གཏོང་དགོས་པ་ཡིན།

ལོ་ཉིས་སྟོང་ལྔ་བརྒྱའི་གོང་ནས་སྟོན་པ་སངས་རྒྱས་བཅོམ་ལྡན་འདས་ཀྱིས་འཛམ་གླིང་འདི་དང་། སྟོང་གསུམ་གྱི་སྟོང་ཆེན་པོའི་ཕྱིའི་འཇིག་རྟེན་གྱི་ཁམས་དང་། ནང་བཅུད་ཀྱི་སེམས་ཅན། བར་སྣང་གི་རླུང་ཁམས་སོགས་འཇིག་རྟེན་བཀོད་པའི་ཆགས་ཚུལ་སོགས་ནང་ཆོས་ཀྱིས་གཞུང་ནས་གསུང་པ་མང་པོ་ཞིག་དེང་སང་གི་ཚན་རིག་པས་བརྟག་དཔྱད་བྱས་ཏེ་ཤེས་ཚོར་བྱུང་ནས། ཧ་ལས་ངོགས་བྱེད་ཀྱི་ཡོད་ཀྱང་། ནང་པས་དེ་ཚོར་གལ་ཆེ་མི་འཛིན་པར། དེ་ལས་འགྲོ་བ་མི་རྣམས་གཞན་ཕན་སྙིང་རྗེ་ཆེན་པོའི་བསླབ་བསྒོམས་སྦྱང་རྒྱུ་དེ་གལ་གནད་ཆེ་བ་ཅིས་ཀྱི་ཡོད།

དེང་སང་ཆུ་རྙོགས་མ་ཆགས་པའི་རྒྱུན་གྱི་མིའི་འཕྲོད་བསྟེན་དང་། སྲོག་ཆགས་མང་པོ་ཞིག་ལ་གནོད་སྐྱོན་ཡོང་གི་ཡོད་པ་དེ་དག་ལོ་བརྒྱ་ཕྲག་རྗེན་ནས་སྟོན་པ་བཅོམ་ལྡན་འདས་ཀྱིས་ཆུ་རྙོགས་བཟོ་མི་ཚོག་པའི་འདུལ་བའི་བཅའ་ཁྲིམས་གཏན་འབེབས་གནང་ཡོད་པ་དང་། དེ་བཞིན་ཐ་ན་གསང་སྤྱོད་རྒྱབ་རྟིང་ལས་ཡན་ལའང་བཅའ་ཁྲིམས་གཏན་འབེབས་གནང་བ་དེ་དག་རང་བྱུང་ཁམས་སྲུང་སྐྱོབ་དགོས་པར་གལ་གནད་ཆེན་པོ་ཅིས་གནང་བ་ཞིག་རེད།

ནང་ཆོས་ནས་རང་བྱུང་ཁམས་དར་ཁྱབ་ཡོང་རྒྱུར་ཤུགས་གནོན་སྟོན་པ་མ་ཟད། ནང་ཆོས་ཀྱིས་རང་བྱུང་ཁམས་ལ་དཔེ་མཚོན་སྦྱར་ནས་བསླབ་བྱ་མང་པོ་རྒྱབ་ཀྱི་ཡོད་པ་རེད། དཔེར་ན།

རྙོགས་མའི་བཟིང་བུ་ཞིག་དཀྲུགས་ན་འདམ་ཡོད་པས་གསལ་བར་མི་རུང་བ་བཞིན་སེམས་

ཀྱང་། དེ་བཞིན་སྐོགས་མར་གནས་པ་ཡིན། གལ་ཏེ་གཙང་ཞིང་འཛམ་པའི་རྫོང་བུ་ཞིག་མ་དཀྲུགས་པར་གང་ཟག་གི་ཆུའི་ནང་གི་རྡོ་དང་། ༡། འགྲན་བུ། དྭངས་དཀར་སོགས་གསལ་བར་མཐོང་བ་བཞིན་སེམས་ཀྱང་དེ་བཞིན་ཞི་བདེར་གནས།

མི་ཏོག་པདྨ་དེ་བཞིན་ཤིན་ཏུ་དང་། ནང་པ་གཉིས་ཀྱིས་ཉོན་མོངས་དུག་གསུམ་གྱི་མ་འགོས་པར་ཞེས་བྱ་ཡོན་ཏན་གྱི་དཔེ་མཚོན་དུ་ཅེས་ཏེ་ཆ་ཚེར་འཛིན་གྱི་ཡོད་པ་རེད། དཔེར་ན།

མི་ཏོག་པདྨ་སྔོན་པོ་དང་། དམར་པོ། དཀར་པོ་སོགས་འགའ་ཤས་འདམ་ཆུའི་ནང་སྐྱེས་ཏེ་ཡར་ཐོན་མ་ཐུབ་པར་འདམ་ཆུ་དེའི་ནང་བསིམས་ནས་ཟད་ཀྱི་ཡོད་པ་རེད། དེའི་ནང་ནས་མི་ཏོག་པདྨ་འགའ་ཤས་ཡར་ཐོན་ཏེ་འདམ་མ་གོས་པར་གཙང་ཞིང་དྲི་ཞིམ་དང་ལྡན་པ་ཞིག་ཡོད་པ་རེད།

དེ་བཞིན་བཅོམ་ལྡན་འདས་ཀྱི་གསུང་ཆོས་ནང་། སྟག་དང་གླུ་ཚིག། སེང་གེ་སོགས། དཔེ་མཚོན་དུ་སྦྱར་ནས་བསླབ་བྱ་མང་པོ་གནང་ཡོད་པ་རེད། དཔེར་ན།

ཡིག་ཆ་འགའ་ཤས་ནང་ཁོང་གི་སེང་གེའི་ངར་སྒྲ་ལྟ་བུ་སྒྲོག་ཆགས་འབུ་བསྲིང་ཆུང་དུ་ཙམ་ཞང་གཏོད་འཚོ་བྱེད་མི་ཉན་པའི་བསླབ་བྱ་གསུང་གི་ཡོད་པ་རེད།

ཚེས་ཐ་སྐོ་ནས་སྒྲིག་ཆགས་ཀྱི་རིགས་འགའ་ཞིག་འཚོ་གནས་ཐུབ་མིན་གྱི་ཉེན་ཁ་ཡོད་པ་དང་། སྒྲིག་ཆགས་རྣམས་མེད་པར་འགྱུར་ན་འཛམ་གླིང་སྣོད་བཅུད་ཀྱི་ནུས་པ་ཉམས་ཆགས་འགྲོ་གི་རེད། ནང་ཆོས་ཀྱི་དཔེ་ཆའི་ནང་། མི་དང་རི་དྭགས་ཕན་ཚུན་བརྟེན་བྱུང་གི་འབྲེལ་བ་ཡོད་པ་རེད། ཅེས་གསལ་ཡོད། དབྱིན་ཡུལ་གྱི་རྒྱལ་ས་ལོན་ཊོན་དུ་ཡོད་དུ་ཡོད་པའི་ པ་ལི་ཡི་གེའི་ཚོགས་པ་ནས་. ཁུད་ད་ཀ་པ་ཐ་ (Khuddakapatha) ཞེས་པའི་དཔེ་ནས་གཤམ་གྱི་ཚིགས་བཅད་འདི་བཞིན་ཟུར་བཏོན་གནང་ཡོད།

སྐྱེ་མ་ཊ་ཀ་རྣམས་ནགས་སུ་ཚེར་གྲོག་དང་།
ཁྱེད་ཅག་མེད་ཚེ་ནགས་ཚལ་སྟོང་བར་ཟད།
དེ་རྗེས་ཁྱེད་ལའང་གནས་ཡུལ་སྟོང་འགྱུར་བས།
དེ་ཕྱིར་ནགས་རྣམས་སྐྱབ་ཕྱིར་མཚོ་བསམས་མོང་།

ནང་ཆོས་ནི་དུས་རྟག་ཏུ་འཛམ་བུ་གླིང་འདིའི་རིག་གནས་ཀུན་ནས་ཕྱུག་པོས་ར་ཆེན་པོ་ཞིག་ཏུ་གནས་ཡོད། དཔེར་ན། མེ་ཏོག་པདྨ་དེ་རྩི་ཤིང་ཀུན་ནས་ཕྲ་མཆོག་ཏུ་འགྱུར་བ་བཞིན་ཡིན།

ནང་པའི་བསྟན་བཅོས་ཚང་མའི་ནང་སྟོན་པ་བཅོམ་ལྡན་འདས་ནགས་ཚལ་དུ་ཚལ་གྱི་ཕྲོག་འོག་ཏུ་སྐུ་བལྟམས་པར་བཤད་ཡོད། ལོ་རྒྱུས་ལ་གཞིགས་ན་ཁོང་འཁྲུངས་མ་ཐག་གོམ་བདུན་སྤོས་ནས་མེ་ཏོག་པདྨ་བདུན་འཁྲུངས་པ་རེད། ཛམྦུ་ནི་ཡི་ཤིང་གི་གྲིབ་བསིལ་འོག་གཞོན་ནུའི་དུས་ཀྱི་ཏིང་ངེས་འཛིན་ལ་སྒོམ་པའི་སྐབས་དེའི་གཡས་གཡོན་དུ་ཤིང་དེ་ ཧིང་ ༨༥༠ ཙམ་ཡོད།

དེ་རྗེས་བྱང་ཆུབ་ལྗོན་ཤིང་གི་ཡལ་འདབ་རྒྱས་པའི་འོག་སྟོན་པ་སངས་རྒྱས་ཀྱི་གོ་འཕང་བརྙེས་པ་རེད། བྱང་ཆུབ་ཀྱི་ལྗོན་ཤིང་དེ་བཞིན་ནང་པར་རྩ་ཆེན་ཡིན་ཙམ་མ་ཟད། ཕྱི་རོལ་ལ་སུ་ཞིགས་པའི་ཆོས་ལུགས་པ་རྣམས་ཀྱིས་ཀྱང་རྩ་ཆེར་རྩིས་པ་རེད།

དཔེ་མཚོན་དེ་དག་ལས་ང་ཚོས་རྩི་ཤིང་འདི་རིགས་ཆོས་ཀྱིས་སྲུང་སྐྱོབ་བྱེད་དགོས་པ་མངོན་ཐུབ་པ་ཡིན། གང་ཡིན་ཟེར་ན། དེ་དག་ནི་སྟོན་པ་སངས་རྒྱས་བཅོམ་ལྡན་འདས་ཀྱི་མཛད་པ་རྣམས་ཐར་མཚོན་ཐུབ་པའི་དཔེ་མཚོན་རྩ་ཆེན་ཤ་སྟག་ཤིག་རེད། དད་ལྡན་རྣམས་དེ་ལ་ཆེད་མངགས་གནོད་འཚེ་བྱ་མི་རིགས་པ་ཡིན།

ཉམས་ཞིབ་བྱེད་མཁན་ཚོར་ཁྱད་ཚོར་པོ་ཞིག་ཤེས་རྟོགས་ཡོང་རྒྱུར་རང་བྱུང་ཁམས་ལ་འགྲེལ་བཤད་རྒྱབ་སྟངས་ཕྱོགས་གཉིས་ནས་བྱེད་ཀྱི་ཡོད། དངོས་མཐོང་གི་འགྲེལ་བརྗོད་གཅིག་དང་ཕྱོགས་རི་འགག་པའི་འགྲེལ་བརྗོད་གཅིག་བཅས་ཡོད།

དེ་དག་ང་ཚོས་རྒྱ་གར་བྱང་ཕྱོགས་ཀྱི་ཛོང་ཁག་ཞིག་གི་རང་བྱུང་ཁམས་ཀྱི་འཁོར་ཡུག་གི་གནས་དང་ཡུན་ལས་ལེན་པ་ཡིན་གསིས། དེ་དག་སྣ་ཚོགས་ཀྱི་ནུས་པ་ཁྱད་འཕགས་ཅན་གྱི་རྟེན་འབྱུང་ལས་བྱུང་བ་ཞིག་ཀྱང་ཡིན། ཐ་མོའི་ནང་པ་རྣམས་རང་བྱུང་རིག་པར་དགའ་སོས་ཡོད་ས་ཞིག་ནི་ངེས་པར་ཡིན།

དེ་ཡང་སྟོན་པས་མདོ་སུ་ཏ་ནི་པ་ཏ་ལས་རྩི་ཤིང་དེ་དག་གི་བརྒྱུད་ལ་རིགས་མི་འདྲ་བ་རྣམ་པ་ཇི་ཙམ་འདུས་ཡོད་པ་སོགས་དངོས་སུ་མངོན་ནུས་པ་རྣམས་བདག་ཅག་གིས་རྟོགས་པར་བྱ་དགོས།

དེ་བཞིན་འབུ་དང་། སྨུག་པའི་འབུ། གྲོག་མ་སོགས་ཀྱང་རིགས་མི་འདྲ་བ་ཇི་ཙམ་ལས་བརྩུས་ཡོད་པ་རྣམས་ཀྱང་ཤེས་དགོས་པ་ཡིན།

ཡུལ་ལྗོངས་ཀྱི་མཐའ་འཁོར་ལ་རྒྱན་ཞིང་རྡོ་ཚིགས་དང་མེ་ཏོག་སོགས་མཛེས་ཞིང་བརྗིད་ཆགས་སུ་གནས་པའི་དབུས་ པའི་ཁྲུ་ཚིགས་ཀྱི་མཐར་ལ་རབ་བྱུང་དང་། ཞོལ་ཆེན་གནས་ཡོད།

ཡུལ་ལྗོངས་ཀྱི་བཀོད་པའི་བཤད་པར། འབྲས་བུ་འཐོག་པའི་ས་གཞི་ལས་ཅི་ཞིང་རྣམས་ལ་མེ་ཏོག་བཀྲ་བ་མིན་ཞིང་ཞེས་དང་། ཀླུང་པོ་དང་། བ་ཀླུང་། ཤ་བ། གཡག སེང་གེ་དང་། སེ་རུ། དེ་རྗེས་རྩག གཟིག་ནག་པོ། དོམ་ལ་སོགས་རི་དྭགས་འདུ་མིན་མང་པོ་ཡོད།

འཛམ་གླིང་ནང་མིའི་གྲངས་འབོར་ཆེས་འཕར་དང་། དེ་དག་གིས་མི་ཤེས་པའི་མཚོངས་སེམས་དང་། འདོད་ཛམ། འཛམ་གླིང་གི་ས་གཞིར་གུས་བཀུར་ཆུང་བ་སོགས་ཀྱིས་རྐྱེན་པས་ཡིད་དགའ་བའི་ཛུ་མ་ར་དེ་དག་དུག་གི་ང་བོར་འགྱུར་ཏེ། རང་བྱུང་རིག་པ་ལ་ཡར་རྒྱས་བྱུང་མེད། དེ་ལྟ་བུའི་རང་བྱུང་གི་ཡོན་ཏན་ལ་བརྡར་བཤིག་གཏོང་མཁན་རྣམས་ལ་ནང་པ་སངས་རྒྱས་པ་རྣམས་ཀྱིས་རྒྱབ་གཉེར་ནས་ཡང་བུ་ཐབས་མེད་གཤིས། ཞིགས་བཤད་ཀྱི་ལྟ་གྲུབ་རྒྱས་པར་བྱེད་ཕྱིར་སློབ་གཉེར་བྱེད་མཁན་དང་། མ་འོངས་པའི་མི་རབས་རྣམས་ཀྱི་ཆེད། དེ་དག་གལ་ཆེར་རྩིས་མཐོང་བྱེད་མཁན་ཚོས་དེ་ལ་ང་བཀོལ་བྱེད་ཀྱི་རེད།

ནང་ཚོས་ཀྱིས་རང་བྱུང་གི་ལྟ་བ་ལ་རྟོགས་ཞིབ་དུ། ང་ཚོས་ཐབས་རྡོ་ཚོགས་ཀྱིས་གསར་སྒྲུབ་བྱས་པ་དང་། བསླབ་བྱ་ཕྱོགས་བསྒྲིགས་བྱས་ཡོད་པ་མ་ཟད། དུས་ཡུན་ཐུང་ངུའི་ནང་རང་བྱུང་ཁམས་ལ་གནོད་པ་ཇི་ཙམ་བཀལ་ཡོད་པ་ཡང་ཤེས་ཐུབ། དེ་ནི་གནས་ཚུལ་མང་པོ་ཤེས་རྟོགས་བྱུང་བ་ཞིག་དང་དེའི་ཐོག་ཉམས་ཞིབ་བྱ་རྒྱུ་དེ་ཛ་དྲག་པོ་ཞིག་ཡིན་པ་དང་། དེ་དག་ལས་ལྷག་ཡོད་པར་དེའི་གོར་སློབ་སྦྱོང་བྱེད་མཁན་རྣམས་ལ་ཤེས་ཡོན་གྱི་མཐུན་རྐྱེན་འཛོམས་པོ་སྤྲོད་དགོས་པ་ཡིན།

ང་ཚོའི་ངོས་ནས་ཆེས་ཟ་མའི་དུས་ནས་དར་ཁྱབ་བྱུང་བའི་ནང་ཚོས་ཀྱི་གླེགས་བམ་ནང་གསུངས་པ་རྣམས་རང་བྱུང་ཁམས་ཀྱི་སྲུང་སྐྱོབ་ལ་ཕན་ནུས་ཅན་ཞིག་དང་། ཡང་དག་པ་ཞིག་ཡིན་པའི་སྒོ་ནས། དེའི་གནད་དོན་རྣམས་ཐོངས་སུ་ཕྱུང་ཐུབ་པ་བྱེད་དགོས།

ང་ཚོས་ལས་དོན་འདི་དག་གི་འབྲས་བུ་རྣམས་གཞན་གྱི་སྔོན་དུ་བཞུགས་ནས་འཁོར་ཡུག་ཀུན་སྲུང་རིག་པར་བརྟེན་ནས་མ་ཤེས་པ་རྣམས་ཤེས་པར་བྱ་རྒྱུ་དང་། འདོད་ཛམ་ཀྱི་ལྟ་ཕན་སེམས་ཀྱིས་མེད་པར་བཟོས། སེམས་ཅན་ཐམས་ཅད་ལ་བྱམས་པ་དང་སྙིང་རྗེའི་ལམ་ནས་འཇིག་བརྟེན་སྟོད་ཀྱི་ཁམས་ལ་རྩིས་མཐོང་ཡོད་ཐབས་བྱ་དགོས་པ་ཡིན་ནོ།།

༄༅། ད་རྩའི་འཁོར་ཡུག་གི་གནས་སྟངས་དང་མ་འོངས་པའི་དགོས་མཁོ།

ཛ་སྦྲད། ཞེ་ཏུན།

༄༅ འདས་པའི་ལོ་ངོ་བཅུ་ཕྲག་གསུམ་རིང་འཛམ་གླིང་འདིར་ཛར་མ་བྱུང་བའི་གང་ཅིའི་ཡར་ཐོན་
བྱུང་ཡོད་རེད། ཐོན་བསྐྱེད་ཀྱི་དངོས་རྫས་ཁྱོན་འབོར་ཤིན་ཏུ་ཆེ་བ་ཡོངས་སུ་ཐྱུད་དང་སྤྱད་བཞིན་
ཡིན་པ་དང་། རིམ་འགྲོས་འདི་ནི་གལ་འགངས་ཅན་གྱི་སྒྲུག་འཚོའི་ལས་སྤྱོད་ཀྱི་རང་བཞིན་རྣམས་
དང་ཕྱི་ཁམས་འཁོར་ཡུག་གི་རང་བཞིན་ལ་ཕན་གནོད་འབྲེལ་བ་ཞིག་རེད། འདི་དག་ལས་འགྱུར་
འགྲོས་ཁ་ཤས་ལ་བརྟེན་ནས་སླར་ཡང་བསྐྱར་གསོ་བྱེད་ཐབས་བྲལ་བའི་ཚབས་ཆེའི་མཐའ་འབྲས་མང་
པོ་ཞིག་འཛམ་གླིང་འདིར་ཡོང་སྲིད་པའི་ཐད་ལ་སེམས་ངལ་ཅི་ཆེ་ཡོད་བཞིན་རེད།

འགྱུར་འགྲོས་ཀྱི་རིམ་ཚད་དང་ད་བར་འགྱུར་ལྡོག་ཕྱིན་ཟིན་པའི་གནས་ཚུལ་ = མས་
མཚོན་བྱེད་དཔེ་གྲངས་དུ་མ་ལས་ཤེས་ཐུབ།

ལོ་རེ་བཞིན་ཞིང་ས་དང་རྩྭ་ཁ་ཅན་གྱི་ཐང་ས་རྒྱ་ཁྱོན་ཧེག་ཏར་ས་ཡ་ཞི་ཕྲ་ཐམ་པ་བྱེ་ཐང་དུ་
འགྱུར་བ་དང་། ས་བཅུད་ཆུ་རླུང་གིས་འཁྱེར་བ་དང་། ཞིང་ས་མ་ཡིན་པའི་ཆེད་དུ་སྤྱོད་རྒྱུར་
བྱེད་པ། གཞན་ཡང་རྐྱེན་གཞན་མང་པོ་ལ་བརྟེན་ནས་ས་གཞིའི་ཐོན་བསྐྱེད་ནུས་བཅུད་གཏན་མེད་

དུ་གཏོང་བཞིན་རེད།

ལོ་རེ་བཞིན་དྲོད་སའི་ཤིང་ནགས་རྒྱ་ཁྱོན་ཧེག་ཏར་ས་ཡ་བཅུ་གཉིས་ཙམ་བརླག་ཏུ་འགྲོ་བཞིན་རེད།

ལོ་རེ་བཞིན་ནུས་བཅུད་ཅན་གྱི་ཞིང་ས༔ ཏྲི་ཚད་ཁྱོན་ཏོན་ཞེར་འབུམ་ཉི་ཤུ་རྩ་ལྔ་ཆུ་རླུང་གིས་འཁྱེར་འདེད་བྱེད་བཞིན་རེད།

ལོ་རེ་བཞིན་རང་བྱུང་གཏེར་ཁ་འདོན་སྤྲུག་ཆེད་ས་རྡོ་ཏྲི་ཚད་ཁྱོན་ཏོན་ཞེར་འབུམ་སུམ་སྟོང་ཐམ་པ་ཕྱིར་འདོན་བྱེད་བཞིན་རེད།

ཕྱི་ལོ་ ༡༩༨༠ ནས་ ༡༩༨༥ བར་ཆུའི་བེད་སྤྱོད་འཕར་ཆ་སོང་བ་ཀི་ལོ་མི་ཏར་ཚད་གསུམ་གྲུ་བཞི་མ་ ༣༠༠༠ ནས་ ༣༧༥༠ བར་ཕྱིན་ཡོད།

ཚོང་ཟུར་བྱེད་པའི་འཕྲུལ་འཁོར་ཆི་རྫས་ཀྱི་མཁོ་སྤྱོད་དེང་སང་ལོ་རེ་བཞིན་མེ་ཏེ་རིག་ཏོན་ས་ཡ་ ༧༥༠༠ སོར་བྱེད་ཀྱི་ཡོད་པ་དང་། འདི་ནི་ལོ་ཉི་ཤུའི་གོང་ལས་ཉིས་ལྡབས་ཕལ་ཆེར་རེད།

ལོ་རེ་བཞིན་གཙོ་བོ་ཡར་རྒྱས་འགྲོ་བཞིན་པའི་རྒྱལ་ཁབ་རྣམས་དང་། ལྷག་པར་གྲོང་གསེབ་ས་ཁུལ་ཁག་ཏུ་ཁྱིམ་ཚང་གི་མཁོ་སྤྱོད་ཆེད་མེ་ཤིང་ཁྱོན་ཚད་གསུམ་གྲུ་བཞི་མ་མི་ཏར་ཐེར་འབུམ་གཉིས་སོར་སྤྱད་ཟད་འགྲོ་བཞིན་རེད།

རླངས་འཁོར་མོ་ཏར་རིགས་ ༡༩༥༠ ལོར་གྲངས་ཁྱོན་ས་ཡ་ལྔ་བཅུ་སོར་ཡོད་པ་ལས་ ༡༩༨༧ ལོར་ས་ཡ་ ༤༡༠ ཐུག་ཏུ་འཕར་ཆ་ཕྱིན་ཡོད་རེད།

གྲངས་འཕར་ཀ་ལས་ཆེ་ཤོས་དེ་ནི་མི་འབོར་རེད། འཛམ་གླིང་གི་མི་འབོར་ཐེར་འབུམ་དང་པོ་དེ་ཕྱི་ལོ་ ༡༨༠༠ ལོ་སྟོད་ལ་ཐོན་ཅིང་། དེ་ནས་ལོ་བརྒྱ་ཐམ་པའི་རྗེས་ལ་ཐེར་འབུམ་གཉིས་པ་ཐོན། དེ་རྗེས་ལོ་ ༣༠ མཇུག་ཏུ་ཐེར་འབུམ་གསུམ་པ་དང་། དེ་ནས་ ༡༩༦༠ ནས་ ༡༩༧༥ བར་ལོ་བཅོ་ལྔའི་ནང་ལ་ཐེར་འབུམ་བཞི་པ་དེ་ཐོན་པ་རེད། དུས་རབས་འདིའི་རྫོགས་མཚམས་ལ་མི་གྲངས་ཐེར་འབུམ་དྲུག་སོར་ཐོན་གྱི་རེད།

གང་ཅིའི་འཕར་ཆ་དང་མཁོ་སྤྱོད་ཀྱི་གྲངས་ཅིས་འཛུགས་སུ་རུང་བ་འདི་དག་ལ་བསམ་ཚོ་བསམ་པར་དཀའ་བའི་གནས་སུ་གྱུར་ཡོད། འཛམ་བུའི་ས་གླིང་འདི་ཚོད་ལས་བརྒལ་བའི་བཀོལ་སྤྱོད་ལོག་པ་དུ་མའི་འོག་ཏུ་ཚུད་ཡོད་པ་ནི་ཧ་ཅང་གསལ་པོ་རེད། ས་གླིང་དབྱིག་གཏུབ་བྱེད་པ། འབུར་འཇོམས་བྱེད་པ། གཞོངས་བཀང་བྱེད་པ། ནང་བཅུད་བཅོར་དབྱུང་བྱེད་པ། ཀམ་ཞྲེངས་གཏོང་བ། ཆུ་ལོག་ཀྱིལ་བ། ནགས་ཚལ་གྱི་སྐྱི་བགས་ཁྱོན་ཆེ་བཤུ་བ་བཅས་ལས་ད་ཆ་ས་གཞིའི་རང་བྱུང་བསྐྱར་གསོའི་ནུས་པའང་ཚད་མཐར་གཏུགས་ཟིན་པ་ལྟ་བུར་གྱུར་ཡོད།

རྩམ་བྲིས་འདིར་ལེ་ཚན་གསུམ་ཡོད། ལེ་ཚན་དང་པོའི་ནང་རླུང་དང་ཆུ་དང་ས་

དང་ཞིང་ནགས་བཅས་ཀྱི་ཐོག་ལ་དཔྱད་པ་མདོར་བསྡུས་ཞིག་བྱས་ཡོད། འདི་དག་ནི་ཕྱིའི་འཁོར་ཡུག་ཅོམ་བྱེད་ཀྱི་ཆ་གཙོ་བོ་རྣམས་ཡིན་ཞིང་། སྲོག་ལྡན་རིགས་ཆུས་པ་དང་། ཁྱབ་འཕེལ་ལ་མེད་དུ་མི་རུང་བའི་འཁོར་ཡུག་གི་ཆ་རྣམས་རེད། དེ་ཚན་གཉིས་པས་རང་བྱུང་འཁོར་ཡུག་ཉམས་བརླག་གི་ལམ་ཕྱོགས་ལས་ཟློག་བྱེད་ཀྱི་དམིགས་བསམ་ཐབས་བྱུས་རིགས་དང་། དཔལ་འབྱོར་དང་གྲིག་འཛུགས་ཀྱི་ལམ་ནས་ཐབས་བྱུས་ཞིབ་ཕྲ་མང་པོ་ཡང་ཁོངས་ནས་ཁ་ཤས་ཀྱི་འགྲེལ་བཤད་བྱས་ཡོད།

དེ་ཚན་གསུམ་པས་སྲོག་ལྡན་འཚོ་བྱེད་ཀྱི་གང་ཅིའི་མཐུད་རྐྱེན་ཡར་རྒྱས་ཆེད་ཐབས་བྱུས་དང་ལས་རིགས་གང་དང་གང་ལ་བསམ་གཞིགས་དང་ལག་བསྟར་དགོས་སྐོར་དང་། འཁོར་ཡུག་ལ་གནོད་སྐྱོན་མི་འགྲོ་བའི་ས་ནས་རང་བྱུང་ཐོན་རྫས་རྣམས་ལ་ཐབས་མཁས་དང་རྒྱུ་མཚན་ལྡན་པས་ཐོངས་སྤྱོད་བྱ་ཚུལ། མདོར་ན་སྲོག་ལྡན་འཚོ་ཐབས་ལ་བསམ་འཆར་འགའ་ཤས་བཅས་བཀོད་ཡོད།

ཡ་རབས་བཟང་སྤྱོད་ཀྱི་སྤྱོད་ཚུལ་སྙིང་རྗེ་དང་བཟོད་པ། སྲོག་ལྡན་ཡོངས་ལ་བརྩེ་སྐྱོང་བྱེད་པ་སོགས་ལ་ངེས་པར་བདག་སྐྱོང་དང་གཅེས་སྲུང་དགོས་པའི་འབོད་སྐུལ་ཤུགས་ཆེ་དང་། དེ་བཞིན་དུ་དམིགས་བསལ་ཐབས་བྱུས་ཇི་ཡོད་རྣམས་ཀྱི་ཉིང་། ད་ལྟ་དང་མ་འོངས་པའི་མི་རབས་ཡོངས་ཀྱི་ཆེད་ས་གཞིའི་རང་བྱུང་ཐོན་རྫས་རྣམས་ལ་གཅེས་སྲུང་བདག་སྐྱོང་ཆེད་འཛུགས་ཐོག་གི་ཐག་གཅོད་བྱ་ཕྱོགས་བཅས་ཀྱི་ཐད་ལ་འབོད་སྐུལ་དང་བཅས་ཏེ་ཅོམ་ཕྱིས་འདི་མཇུག་རྫོགས་བྱས་ཡོད།།

འཁོར་ཡུག་གི་གནས་སྟངས།

༄༅ ཕྱི་ཁམས་འཁོར་ཡུག་གི་གནས་སྟངས་ཇི་འདྲ་ཞིག་ཏུ་གྱུར་ཡོད་མེད་སྐོར་ལ་དེང་སང་གསལ་བསྒྲགས་དང་ཡིག་ཆ་མང་པོ་ཐོབ་ཀྱི་ཡོད། ༡༩༧༢ ལོར་སུ་ཡི་ཊེན་གྱི་རྒྱལ་ས་སེ་ཀྲོག་ཧོམ་ལ་མིའི་ཕྱི་ཁམས་འཁོར་ཡུག་སྐོར་ལ་རྒྱལ་སྤྱིའི་ཚན་ཚོགས་ཞེས་པ་དེ་ཚོགས་ནས་ལོ་ངོ་བཅུ་སོང་རྗེས་ ༡༩༨༢ ལོར་རྒྱལ་སྤྱིའི་ཕྱི་ཁམས་འཁོར་ཡུག་ཐོག་མཛད་འཆར་ United Nations Environment Programme, UNEP ཞེས་པ་དེས་འཁོར་ཡུག་གི་གནས་སྟངས་སྐོར་ལ་བསྐྱར་ཞིབ་ཚོག་ཐོ་རྒྱས་ཞིབ་དོན་གསལ་ཅན་ཞིག་ཕྱིལ་ཡོད། མཛད་འཆར་འདིས་ལོ་རེ་བཞིན་འཁོར་ཡུག་གི་གནས་སྐོར་ལ་གལ་ཆེའི་བརྗོད་གཞི་སྣ་ཚོགས་དཔར་བསྐྲུན་བྱེད་ཀྱི་ཡོད་རེད། དེ་བཞིན་དུ་རྒྱལ་སྤྱི་དང་རྒྱལ་ཁབ་སོ་སོ་སོགས་གཞན་མང་པོ་ནས་ཀྱང་གནས་ཚུལ་འདི་ཐོག་ཉམས་ཞིབ་དང་གསལ་བསྒྲགས་བྱེད་ཀྱི་ཡོད་རེད། དཔྱད་ཞིབ་དེ་ཚན་དང་པོ་འདིའི་ནང་ལ་ཙ་བའི་འགྱུར་བ་གང་དང་གང་འགྲོ་བཞིན་ཡོད་པ་གསལ་ཁ་ཆེད་སྲོག་འཚོའི་ཆ་རྐྱེན་གལ་འགངས་ཅན་ཁག་གི་ལས་ཚུལ་དང་རང་བཞིན་སྐོར་ལ་གོ་བདེའི་ལམ་ནས་འགྲེལ་བཤད་བྱ་རྒྱུ་ཡིན།

བར་སྣང་རླུང་ཁམས་ཀྱི་ཁྲུས་ཁ།

བར་སྣང་རླུང་ཁམས་ཀྱི་གནས་སྟངས་ཇེ་ཞན་དུ་སོང་བའི་དཀའ་ངལ་མང་པོ་ཞིག་འབྱུང་ཀྱི་ཡོད་རེད། འདི་དག་ནི། དུག་སྣའི་བུན་ཆར་ Acid Rain ཞེས་པ་དང་། ཤིང་སྡོང་རྫས་རླུང་གི་འདུ་བསགས་ Greenhouse Gases ཞེས་པ་དང་། ཨོ་ཛོན་གྱི་གདན་རིམ་འཐོར་ཟད་ Ozone Layer Depletion ཅེས་པ་སོགས་རེད།

དུག་སྣའི་བུན་ཆར་ཞེས་པ་ནི། མུ་ཟི་དང་ན་ཡི་ཏྲོ་ཇན་གཉིས་བར་སྣང་དུ་སྲོག་འཛིན་རླུང་དང་འདུ་འཕྲོད་བྱས་པ་ལས་གྲུབ་པའི་འདུས་རྫས་ཁྱུན་ཆེ་ཁྱབ་བདལ་དུ་གནས་པ་རྣམས་ཆར་སྤྲིན་གཉིས་དང་འགྲོགས་ཤིང་། དེ་ལ་བརྟེན་ནས་དུག་སྣས་བསླད་པའི་གངས་ཆར་ས་ལ་བབས་པ་ལ་ཟེར་བ་རེད། ད་ཆ་རགས་རྩིས་བྱས་ན། མུ་ཟིའི་རྫས་དང་ (Sulphur) ན་ཡི་ཏྲོ་ཇན་ (Nitrogen) གཉིས་ཀྱི་སྲོག་རླུང་འདུས་རྫས་ (Oxides) ལོ་རེར་ཐོན་ས་ཡ་ ༡༨༠ འཕོ་ཐོན་ཡོང་གི་ཡོད། རྫས་རླུང་འདི་དག་འགྱངས་ཐག་དང་མཐོ་ཚད་ཀི་ལོ་མི་ཏར་ ༡༠༠༠ རིང་པ་འཕོ་བསྐྱོད་ཐུབ་ཀྱི་ཡོད་པའང་གསལ་པོར་ཤེས་རྟོགས་ཐུབ་ཡོད། འཕོ་བསྐྱོད་ཀྱི་རིམ་པའི་སྐབས་མུ་ཟི་སྲོག་རླུང་ཉིས་འདུས་ (Sulphur dioxide) རྫས་རླུང་ཞེས་པ་དེ་བར་སྣང་ནས་ལམ་ཚོལ་གསུམ་གྱི་སྒོ་ནས་གཙང་ཟད་དུ་འགྲོ་བ་རེད། འོག་གི་ས་གཞིར་ཐིམ་འདུས་ཀྱིས་གཙང་ཟད་དུ་འགྲོ་བ། ཆར་སྤྲིན་གྱི་ཆུ་རྡུལ་ནང་བཞུ་ཐིམ་གྱིས་གཙང་ཟད་དུ་འགྲོ་བ། སྲོག་འཛིན་རླུང་དང་འདུ་འཕྲོད་ཀྱིས་མུ་ཟིའི་དུག་ཆུའི་ (Sulphuric acid) ངོ་བོར་འགྱུར་བས་གཙང་ཟད་དུ་འགྲོ་བ་བཅས་རེད། འདི་དག་རིམ་བཞིན་ཁ་ཆར་དང་འགྲོགས་ཏེ་ས་ལ་བབ་ཀྱི་ཡོད་རེད། ན་ཡི་ཏྲོར་ཇན་དང་སྲོག་རླུང་འདུས་རྫས་ (Nitrogen oxides) རྣམས་ཀྱང་གོང་བཞིན་འདུས་རྫས་དང་དུག་ཆུའི་ངོ་བོར་སོང་སྟེ་ཁ་ཆར་གྱིས་ས་ལ་འབེབས་ཀྱི་ཡོད་རེད། དེང་སྐབས་ནགས་ཚལ་ཁྱུན་ཆེ་རྩ་མེད་དུ་འགྲོ་བཞིན་ཡོད་པའི་རྐྱེན་རྩ་གཙོ་བོ་ཞིག་དུག་སྣའི་བུན་ཆར་འདི་རེད་ཅེས་བལ་ཆེར་གྱིས་ངོས་འཛིན་བྱེད་ཀྱི་ཡོད་རེད། དེ་བཞིན་དུ་འདི་ལ་བརྟེན་ནས་རིན་ཐང་བྲལ་བའི་མཁར་རྙིང་དང་སྐུ་བརྙན་རྙིང་རིགས་ཁག་རྙིང་ཟད་དུ་འགྲོ་བའི་མགྱོགས་རྐྱེན་བྱེད་ཀྱི་ཡོད། དེར་བརྟེན་ཙུགས་རིགས་རིན་ཆེན་རྡོ་ཚིགས་ལས་གྲུབ་པའི་དངོས་རྙིང་ཟུར་དང་ཤི་འདྲ་བར་བཅའ་དང་གཡའ་ལ་སོགས་པ་ལས་སྲུང་སྐྱོབ་ཆེད་ཚོན་རྩི་ཡང་ཡང་གཏོང་དགོས་སོགས་དཔལ་འབྱོར་གྱི་འགྲོ་སྒྲོན་མ་མང་པོ་གཏོང་དགོས་འགྱུར་བཞིན་ཡོད་རེད།

ཤིང་སྡོང་ཁང་གི་རྫས་རླུང་འདུས་བསགས།

༡༽ སྡང་ཁང་རྫས་རླུང་དེ་ཚན་ཁོངས་ནས་ཀར་བོན་ཌ་ཡི་ཨོག་ས་ཡིཊ (Carbon dioxide)

དང་། ཀར་བོན་མོ་ནོ་ཨོག་ས་ཡིཊ་ (carbonmonoxide) མི་ཐེན་ (Methane) ན་ཡི་ཊོ་རོ་ཛན་དང་སྤྲག་འཛོན་རླུང་གཉིས་ཀྱི་འདུས་རླུང་ཁག་ (Nitrogen oxides) རྣམས་ཀྱི་འདུས་བསགས་འཕར་ཆ་ཅི་ཆེར་འགྲོ་བཞིན་ཡོད་པས། འབྱུང་བའི་འགྱུར་འགྲོས་རྫིང་ཁང་འགྱུར་འབྲས་ (Greenhouse Effect) ཞེས་པ་ལ་བརྟེན་ནས་གནམ་གཤིས་ཀྱི་ཚ་དྲོད་ཇེ་མཐོར་འགྲོ་སྲིད། དེ་དག་ལས་ཀྱང་ཀར་བོན་ཌ་ཡི་ཨོག་ས་ཡིཊ་ཐོན་འཕེལ་ཆེ་ཤོས་རེད། ༡༩༥༠ ནས་ ༡༩༨༠ བར་འདིའི་འཕར་ཆ་ལོ་རེ་བཞིན་བརྒྱ་ཆ་བཞིས་གོང་འཕེལ་དུ་འགྲོ་བཞིན་རེད། བར་སྣང་ལ་གོང་གསལ་རྫས་རླུང་ཁག་འཕེལ་བསགས་ལ་བརྟེན་ནས་ཞིང་གསོ་ཁང་གི་འགྱུར་འགྲོས་ལྟར་བར་སྣང་གི་དྲོད་ཚད་འཕེལ་འགྱུར་གཏོང་གི་ཡོད་རེད། ༡༩༨༥ ལོར་ཨ་ལི་ཀྲི་རི་ཡར་རྫིང་ཁང་རྫས་རླུང་དང་གནམ་གཤིས་འགྱུར་འགྲོས་སྐོར་ལ་རྒྱལ་སྤྱིའི་ཚད་རིག་གི་ཀུན་ཚོགས་ཞིག་གི་སྐབས་སོས་མཐུན་དང་ཞིབ་རྩོམ་བྱུང་གསལ། གལ་སྲིད་བར་སྣང་དུ་ཀར་བོན་ཌ་ཡི་ཨོག་ས་ཡིཊ་ཉིས་ལྡབ་ཀྱིས་འཕར་ཆ་བྱུང་ན་ས་སྟེང་གི་ཚ་ཚད་སེན་ཊི་གི་ཊེཊ་ཕྱེད་གཉིས་ནས་ཕྱེད་དང་ལྔའི་བར་འཕར་ཆ་འགྲོ་རྒྱུ་དང་། དེ་ལ་བརྟེན་ནས་རླུང་དང་རྒྱ་མཚོའི་རླབས་སོགས་ལའང་འགྱུར་བ་འགྲོ་རྒྱུ་དང་། དེ་དག་ལ་བརྟེན་ནས་རྒྱ་མཚོའི་ཁ་ཚད་སེན་ཊི་མི་ཊར་ ༣༠ ནས་ ༡༩༠ བར་མཐོ་རུ་འགྲོ་རྒྱུ་དང་། འདི་དག་དངོས་བྱུང་རྒྱུར་ན་མཚོ་ཁའི་གྲོང་ཁྱེར་མང་པོ་རིམ་བཞིན་མཚོ་འོག་ཏུ་ནུབ་རྒྱུ་སོགས་གནས་ཚུལ་ཚབས་ཆེ་མང་པོ་འབྱུང་སྲིད་པ་རེད།

ཨོ་ཛོན་གྱི་གདན་རིམ་འཐོར་ཟད་ཀྱི་ཉེན་ཁ།

ཨོ་ཛོན་ནི་ (Ozone) རྫས་སྦྱར་འདུ་འཕྲོད་ལ་ཤིན་ཏུ་མྱུར་བའི་རྫས་རླུང་ཞིག་རེད། འདི་ནི་བར་སྣང་རླུང་ཁམས་ཀྱི་གདན་རིམ་གཉིས་པ་ཁྲབ་བྱེད་རླུང་ཁམས་ (Stratosphere) ཞེས་པའི་ནང་དུ་གདན་རིམ་སྲབ་མོ་ཞིག་ཏུ་འབྱུང་འཛག་གནས་གསུམ་བྱེད་པ་རེད། ཨོ་ཛོན་གྱི་གདན་རིམ་འདིས་ཉི་ཟེར་གྱི་ཚད་མེད་འོད་ཟེར་ (Ultra Violet) ཞེས་པའི་འོད་ཟེར་དེ་ཐིམ་ལེན་བྱེད་ཀྱི་ཡོད་རེད། འོད་ཟེར་འདི་སྲོག་ཆགས་རིགས་ལ་ཕོག་ན་གནོད་ཚབས་ཆེན་པོ་བྱེད་ཀྱི་ཡོད་བརྟེན་གལ་ཏེ་ཨོ་ཛོན་གྱི་གདན་རིམ་འཐོར་ཟད་དུ་སོང་ན་འོད་ཟེར་འདི་རིགས་ས་སྟེང་དུ་ཕོག་རྟིང་གནོད་སྐྱོན་ཅི་ཆེ་ཡོང་རྒྱུ་རེད། བར་སྣང་གི་ཨོ་ཛོན་གྱི་གདན་རིམ་འཐོར་ཟད་གཏོང་མཁན་གཙོ་བོ་ནི་ན་ཡི་ཊོ་རོ་ཛན་གྱི་སྤྲག་རླུང་འདུས་རྫས་གཉིས (NO and NO_2) དང་བར་སྣང་གི་ཆ་རྡུལ་སོགས་རེད། འོད་ཟེར་འདི་ལ་བརྟེན་ནས་ཀན་སར་པགས་ནད་ (Skin Cancer) རིགས་གཉིས་འབྱུང་སྲིད། མེ་ལ་ནོ་མ་ཞེས་པའི་པགས་ནད་མ་ཡིན་པའི་པགས་ནད་ཀན་སར་ལས་ཤི་སྐྱོན་ཕལ་ཆེར་མི་འབྱུང་ཡང་། མེ་ལ་ནོ་མ་ (Melanoma) པགས་ནད་ཀན་སར་ལས་ནི་ནད་

པ་བརྒྱ་ཆ་ ༢༢ ལ་འཆི་རྐྱེན་གཏོང་བ་རེད།

ཚད་མེད་ནད་ཟེར་ཞེས་པ་འདི་སྙིང་དུ་ཕོག་འཕོ་བྱང་དུ་སོང་ན། ས་ངོས་ཀྱི་རྩི་ཤིང་ནགས་ཚལ་ལ་འང་གནོད་སྐྱོན་ཆེན་པོ་གཏོང་ནུས། ཨ་རིའི་ལོ་ཞིབ་ཉམས་ཞིབ་ཚོགས་པ་ཞིག་གི་ཚོག་ཐོར། བར་སྣང་གི་ཨོ་ཛོན་ཉམས་རྒྱུན་ལྟན་བུ་སོར་བའི་ཡུལ་གྱི་ཟ་དམ་གྱི་ཕྱོན་ཐག་བརྒྱ་ཆ་ལྔ་བཅུ་ཟམ་པས་ཞན་པ་འདུག་ཅེས་བཀོད་ཡོད་རེད། དེར་བརྟེན་ཏྲན་ཐོག་ལ་བརྟེན་པའི་དཔལ་འབྱོར་གྱི་སྐྱོང་གུན་འདི་ཤིན་ཏུ་གལ་འགངས་ཆེན་པོའི་གནས་ཚུལ་ཞིག་རེད། ཁྱབ་བྱེད་སྣང་ཁམས་ཀྱི་ཨོ་ཛོན་གདན་རིམ་ལ་ཉམས་འགྱུར་བྱུང་འབྲས་ལས་དྲོད་ཚད་དང་། སྣང་གི་རྒྱུ་བ། ཚ་སྣང་གི་འདུ་གསོག་བཅས་ལ་འང་འགྱུར་བ་ཕྱིན་ཏེ་ས་སྟེང་ཡོངས་ལ་གནམ་གཤིས་ཀྱི་འགྱུར་བ་ཡོང་གི་རེད།

ཆུ་དང་དེའི་བེད་སྤྱོད།

འཛམ་གླིང་ཆུའི་ཁུན་ཚད་རགས་རྩིས་ཀྱི་ཚོ་སི་ཏར་ཚད་གསུམ་གྱི་བཞི་མ་ས་ཡ་ ༡༩༠༠ ཡོད་ཅིང་འདི་ལ་འགྱུར་བ་ཕལ་ཆེར་མེད། འོན་ཀྱང་ཆུ་ཁུན་དེའི་བརྒྱ་ཆ་ ༩༧ རྒྱ་མཚོའི་ཆུ་རེད། བརྒྱ་ཆ་བཅུ་ཟུར་གཅིག་ཙམ་རང་བྱུང་གིས་གཙང་ཆུ་རེད། དེའི་ཆག་འཁྱིལ་རྣམས་འཛམ་གླིང་སྤྱི་བྱུང་གི་མཐོ་ཞབས་གཉིས་སུ་འཁྱགས་རོམ་རོག་སི་ཏར་ ༧༥༠ མཐུག་ཚད་བར་གནས་པ་དང་། བར་སྣང་གི་ཆུ་སྣང་བཅས་ལ་ཡོད། གཙང་ཆུ་ཁུན་ཆུང་འདི་ལས་མེད་པ་དེ་ལ་ཡང་བེད་སྤྱོད་ཐོག་པ་ཡང་ཡང་བཏང་སྟེ་ཆུད་ཟོས་སུ་གཏོང་གི་ཡོད་རེད།

ཆུའི་མཁོ་སྤྱོད།

ཆུའི་མཁོ་སྤྱོད་ཀྱི་རགས་རྩིས་རྟར་ན། ༡༩༨༥ ལོར་ཆུ་བེད་སྤྱོད་བྱས་པ་ཀི་ལོ་སི་ཏར་ཚད་གསུམ་གྱི་བཞི་མ་ ༢༠༠༠ སོར་རེད། དེ་ལས་བརྒྱ་ཆ་ ༧༢ ཞིང་ཆུ། བརྒྱ་ཆ་ ༢༡ བཟོ་གྲྭའི་མཁོ་སྤྱོད། བརྒྱ་ཆ་ ༦ ཁྱིམ་ཚང་ནང་གི་མཁོ་སྤྱོད་ལ་ཕྱིན་ཡོད།

༡༩༦༠ ནས་ ༡༩༨༥ བར་ཞིང་ཆུ་འདྲེན་ཡུལ་ས་ཞིང་གི་འཕར་ཆ་ཧེག་ཏར་ས་ཡ་ ༢༨ ནས་ཧེག་ཏར་ས་ཡ་ ༥༠ བར་ཕྱིན་ཡོད། འོན་ཀྱང་ཞིང་ཆུའི་གྲུབ་འབྲས་ནུས་ཤུགས་དམར་པོ་ལས་ཐོན་ཐུབ་མེད། བརྒྱ་ཆ་ ༢༠ ནས་ ༥༠ བར་མ་གཏོགས་ནུས་ཤུགས་ཐིན་མེད། ཀམ་ཤས་ཆེ་སའི་ས་ཁུལ་དུ་ས་འོག་གི་ཆུ་གཏེར་ལ་སྤྱོད་ཟལ་ཆེ་བའི་རྐྱེན་གྱིས་ཆུའི་ནུས་བཅུད་སྟོངས་ཟད་དུ་ཕྱིན་པ་དང་། ཆུ་འདྲེན་ལས་ལུགས་མི་འཚམ་པར་སྤྱོད་པའི་དབང་གིས་བ་ཚྭ་དང་དུག་ཚྭ་ཅན་དུ་ཤ། །བསྒྱུར་བ་དང་། ཞིང་ས་གཤིན་པོ་རྣམས་ས་ཅང་ཐན་གཤེར་ཅན་དུ་གྱུར་པ་སོགས་བྱུང་ཡོད་རེད།

བཟོ་གྲྭའི་ནང་དུ་ཆུའི་མཁོ་སྤྱོད་ཐད། ཡར་རྒྱས་ཅན་པའི་རྒྱལ་ཁབ་རྣམས་ནང་བཟོ་གྲྭའི་ནང་ཆུའི་འགྲོ་སྤྱོད་ཆུང་དུ་ཕྱིན་ཡོད། གང་ཡིན་ཞེ་ན། ལས་ལུགས་ཡར་རྒྱས་དང་སྤྱད་ཟིན་གྱི་ཆུ་ལ་སྐྱར་ཡང་

སྤྱོད་ཕྱུགས་པ་སོགས་ཀྱི་རྒྱུ་མཚན་གྱིས་རེད། འོན་ཀྱང་ཡར་རྒྱས་འགྲོ་བཞིན་པའི་རྒྱལ་ཁབ་ཁག་ནང་བཟོ་ལས་ཡར་རྒྱས་དང་ཉེན་དུ་ཆུའི་མཁོ་སྤྱོད་ཀྱང་ཚ་རུ་འགྲོ་བཞིན་ཡོད་རེད། རྒྱལ་ཁབ་དེ་དག་ནང་ཆུ་ལ་སྤྱོད་མཁས་ཀྱི་ལས་ཚོལ་ཁག་ཡག་ཡོན་བརྩར་དགོས་ཡོད།

མི་མང་གི་འཕྱང་ཆུ་དང་། གཙང་སྦྲ། བཀལ་འཁྱུད་བཅས་ལ་ཆུ་འགྲོ་བརྒྱ་ཆ་ཤིན་ཏུ་ཆུང་ངུ་ལས་མེད་ཀྱང་། འདི་དག་ནི་འགྲིབ་མི་རིགས་སྤྱིའི་འཚོ་བརྟན་ལ་ཕན་གནོད་ཆེན་པོ་འབྲེལ་བ་ཞིག་རེད། ཡར་རྒྱས་འགྲོ་བཞིན་པའི་རྒྱལ་ཁབ་ཁག་ནང་མི་གྲངས་ཟླ་ཆ་གསུམ་ལ་འཐུང་ཆུ་གཙང་མ་ཐོབ་དཀའི་དཀའ་ཡོད། མི་འབོར་ཐེར་འབུམ་གཉིས་བཅོ་ཆུ་ཡོངས་སུ་སྤྱོད་པ་ལས་བྱུང་བའི་ནད་ཚ་མང་པོའི་ཉེན་ཁའི་འོག་གནས་ཡོད།

ཡར་རྒྱས་འགྲོ་བཞིན་པའི་རྒྱལ་ཁབ་རྣམས་ནང་མི་གྲངས་བཞི་ཆ་གསུམ་ལ་གཞི་རྩའི་གཙང་སྦྲའི་མཐུན་རྐྱེན་རྩ་བ་ནས་མེད།

ཆ་ལ་བཙོག་སྐྱོད་ཀྱི་གནས་ཚུལ།

རྒྱལ་ཁབ་མང་པོའི་ནང་ཁྱིམ་ཁང་གི་བཙོག་ཆུ་དང་། ཞིང་ཆུ་ལས་སྨན་ལུད་སོགས་ཀྱི་རྐྱེན་གྱིས་ས་སྙིང་ཆུ་གཏེར་རྣམས་ཀྱི་བཅུད་ཤུགས་ལ་འགྱུར་བ་ཆེན་པོ་གཏོང་གི་ཡོད་རེད། ད་བཞིན་དུ་གཙང་ཆུ་རྣམས་དང་ས་འོག་གི་ཆུ་རྣམས་སུ་ན་ཡི་ཏེ་རོ་ཛན་ཀྱི་འདུས་རྫས་ཁྱོན་ཚེ་འདུས་བསགས་ཡོང་བཞིན་ཡོད་པའང་སེམས་ངལ་འོས་པའི་གནས་ཚུལ་ཞིག་རེད། ཆུ་ལི་ཏར་གཅིག་ནང་དེ་འདྲའི་འདུས་རྫས་མི་ལི་གྲམ་བཅུ་ལྷག་ཡོད་ཚེ་ཕྱུས་པོར་གནོད་ཉེན་ཡོད་རེད།

ཡར་རྒྱས་འགྲོ་བཞིན་པའི་རྒྱལ་ཁབ་ཕལ་ཆེ་བའི་ནང་གྲོང་པའི་བཙོག་ཆུ་རྣམས་གཙང་པོ་དང་རྒྱུགས་ཆུ་རྣམས་སུ་འདྲེས་ཏེ་རང་བྱུང་ཆུ་གཏེར་དེ་དག་འཐུང་ཆར་མི་རུང་བར་འགྱུར་བཞིན་རེད། . བཟོ་གྲྭ་ཡར་རྒྱས་འགྲོ་རིམ་བཞིན་དུ་ཆུར་བཙོག་སྐྱོད་ཀྱང་ཇེ་ཆེར་འགྲོ་བཞིན་རེད། ཕྱིར་བཟོ་གྲྭས་འཐུང་ཆུར་བཙོག་བསླད་འགོག་ཐབས་ཡང་ལེགས་མང་པོ་བྱུང་ཡོད་ཀྱང་། ཐབས་ཚུལ་དེ་དག་གིས་འགོག་མི་ཐུབ་པའི་དུག་རྫས་མང་པོ་ཇེ་ཞ། །འཕེལ་དུ་འགྲོ་བཞིན་རེད། རགས་ཙམ་བྱས་ན། ལོ་རེར་རྒྱ་མཚོའི་ནང་རྫས་རིགས་འདྲ་མིན་ཁྲིན་ཐེར་འབུམ་ ༣༥ འཕེན་བཞིན་ཡིན་པ་དང་། དེའི་བརྒྱ་ཆ་ ༩༠ གཙང་ཆུ་བརྒྱུད་དེ་ཡོང་གི་ཡོད།

སའི་གནས་སྟངས།

ད་སྔའི་ཆར་འཛམ་གླིང་ཁྱོན་ལ་ཞིང་ས་རུང་བའི་ས་ཁྱོན་ཧེག་ཏར་ཐེར་འབུམ་ཕྱེད་དང་གཉིས་སྐོར་ཡོད། རགས་རྩིས་བྱས་ན། ལོ་རེ་བཞིན་ཞིང་ས་གཡེན་པོ་ཐོན་ཐེར་འབུམ་ ༣༥ རེ་ཙ་བརླག་འགྲོ་བཞིན་རེད། འཛམ་གླིང་ས་ངོས་བརྒྱ་ཆ་ ༤༡ ཐང་སྐམ་པོར་འགྱུར་བཞིན་ཅིང་། ད་ལ་བརྟེན་ནས་མི་འབོར་ས་ཡ་ ༨༥༠ ལྷག་གི་འཚོ་བའི་གནས་སྟངས་ལ་གནོད་སྐྱོན་ཕྱིན་ཡོད། ལོ་རེ་བཞིན་ཧེག་ཏར་ས་ཡ་ཟ་ནས་

བདུན་བར་ཞིངས་ཉུང་བའི་ས་ཁོངས་ནས་བྱེ་ཐང་དུ་འགྱུར་བཞིན་ཡོད།

བྱེ་ཐང་དུ་འགྱུར་གཞིའི་རྒྱུ་རྐྱེན་གཙོ་བོ་ཁག་ནི། རྩྭ་ཁ་ཁག་ལ་སྤྱོད་དྲགས་པ་དང་། ཞིང་ས་ལ་ནང་གསེས་ཆ་ཕྲན་ཕྲུས་དྲགས་པ། ས་འོག་གི་ཆུན་གསེར་ཀུན་ལུད་བྱས་པ། ཞིང་ཆར་བ་ཆུ་དང་དུག་ཆུ་རིགས་ཤས་ཆེས་པ། ཤིང་ནགས་དང་རྩི་ཤིང་རྣམས་མི་ཤིང་སོགས་ཀྱི་ཚོད་བཅད་བཏུབ་མངས་པའི་རྐྱེན་བཅས་རེད།

སའི་སྟུས་ཁ་ཇེ་ཞན་དུ་འགྲོ་བའི་རྒྱུ་རྐྱེན་གཙོ་བོ་ཞི། སའི་ཐུས་བཅུད་ཆུ་རླུང་གིས་འཕྲོར་འདེད་བྱེད་པ་དེ་རེད།

ལྟོན་ཐོག་ཐོན་བསྐྱེད་ལ་ཉམས་རྒྱུད་འགྲོ་བའི་རྐྱེན་རྩ་གཙོ་བོ་ནི། མི་འབོར་གྲངས་འཕེལ་ཚས་ཆར་འགྲོ་བའི་དབང་གིས་རེད། མི་འབོར་གྲངས་འཕེལ་དང་ཟླན་དུ་ས་ཕྱོན་རྒྱ་བསྐྱེད་འགྲོ་རྒྱུ་མེད་པོག། ཐོན་བསྐྱེད་ཀྱི་ཚོད་གཞི་དང་སྟུས་ཁ་སོགས་ལ་ཟུར་ལས་ཀྱང་ཇེ་ཞན་དུ་འགྲོ་བཞིན་རེད།

རྒྱ་ནག་གི་ཡང་ཅེ་གཙང་པོ་དང་རྒྱ་གར་གྱི་ཆུ་མོ་གང་ག་གཉིས་ཀྱིས་ཕོ་རིམ་བཞིན་ལོ་རར་བྱེ་མ་ཕོན་ས་ཡ་ ༡༦༠༠ དང་ ༡༩༥༠ འཁྱེར་འདེད་བྱེད་ཀྱི་ཡོད་པ་ཡ་དཔགས་ཏེ་ཞིང་ས་ཆུ་རླུང་གིས་འཕྱར་འདེད་ཇེ་ཆེས་འགྲོ་བཞིན་ཡོད་པ་མཚོན་ཐུབ་པ་ཞིག་རེད།

ཤིང་ནགས་འཛོམས་འཇིག་དང་། སྲོག་ཆགས་རིགས་ཆད་སོར།

ཚ་དྲོད་ཚ་ལས་ཀྱི་བའི་ཤིང་ནགས་རིགས་ (Tropical Forests)ནི། འགྲོ་བ་མིར་གང་ཅིའི་ཐད་ནས་ཀྱི། །ཤིན་ཏུ་མཁོ་ཕན་ཆེན་པོ་རེད། སྨན་རིགས་བཟོ་གྲྭའི་བརྒྱ་ཆ་ ༥༠ ཙམ་ཤིང་ནགས་འདི་ལས་ཐོན་པ་དང་། གཞན་ཡང་ཀཕེ་ཆེའི་རྨུམ་རིགས། འབྲུག་ས་རིགས། རས་སྟན། ཚོན་རྩི་དང་སྦྱར་རྩི། ཤིང་རྩི་བཅས་ཀྱང་འདི་ལས་འབྱུང་། གཞན་ཡང་ཤིང་ནགས་འདི་ནི་མི་འབོར་ས་ཡ་ ༣༠༠ སོར་གྱི་གནས་ཁང་ལྟ་བུ་དང་། ཁོང་ཚོའི་ལྟོ་ཆས། མེ་ཤིང་། རྫོང་གནས། སྒོ་ཕྱུགས་ཀྱི་ལྟོ་ཆག་བཅས་ཡོངས་རྫོགས་འདི་ལ་བརྟེན་ཡོད། ད་བར་སྲོག་ཆགས་འབུ་སྲིན་རིགས་ས་ཡ་གཅིག་དང་བདུན་འབུམ་སོར་ངོས་འཛིན་ཐུབ་ཡོད་ཅིང་། ཡོངས་གྲགས་ལྟར་ན་སྲོག་ཆགས་རིགས་ས་ཡ་ཟླ་ཉུང་མཐར་ཡོད་པར་འདོད་ཀྱི་ཡོད་པ་དང་། ཚན་རིག་མཁས་པ་མང་པོས་སྲོག་ཆགས་རིགས་ས་ཡ་བཅུ་ལྷག་ཡོད་པར་འདོད་ཀྱི་ཡོད་རེད། སྲོག་ཆགས་རིགས་ཕྱོན་ཆེ་དེ་དག་ལས་བརྒྱ་ཆ་ ༧༥ ལས་མི་ཉུང་བ་ཤིང་ནགས་ཀྱི་རིགས་འདིའི་ནང་གནས་ཡོད་རེད།

སྲོག་ཆགས་རིགས་ཆད་ཀྱི་གནས་ཚུལ་ནི། སྔར་དུས་ཀྱི་ཐོག་མ་ནས་བྱུང་ཡོད་ཀྱང་། དེང་སང་སྲོག་ཆགས་རིགས་ཆད་ཀྱི་འཕར་ཚའི་མགྱོགས་ཚད་ལ་བལྟས་ན་འཇིགས་སྣང་སྐྱེ་འོས་པར་གྱུར་ཡོད།

མཁས་པ་ཁ་ཤས་ནས་དུས་རབས་འདིའི་མཇུག་མཚམས་ལ་སྲོག་ཆགས་རིགས་ས་ཡ་གཅིག་ཙམ་སོར་གཏན་ནས་རིགས་ཆད་དུ་འགྲོ་རྒྱུའི་མ་འོངས་སྔོན་བརྗོད་བྱས་ཡོད་རེད། སྲོག་ཆགས་ཕྱོན་ཆེ་རིགས་ཆད་དགོས་པའི་རྒྱུ་རྐྱེན་གཙོ་བོ་ཞིག་ཡི། སྲོག་ཆགས་དེ་དག་གི་གནས་ཤིང་ནགས་ལྟ་བུ་རྣམས་བསམ་མེད་ཀྱིས་རྩོར་བཅོམ་བྱེད་པ་

དེ་རེད། ཞིང་ནགས་སྐྱོར་བཙོམ་ནི། ཞིང་སའི་ཆེད་ཞིང་ནགས་བྲེག་གཅོད་དང་སྲེག་སྲར་བྱེད་པ། འཕོར་ལམ་བཟོ་བ། གཞིས་ཆགས་འཛུགས་བསྐྲུན་བྱེད་པ། ཆུ་རགས་བཟོ་བ་སོགས་ལ་བརྟེན་ནས་བྱུང་བའི་གནས་ཚུལ་ཞིག་རེད། དེང་སྐབས་ཞིང་ནགས་བསྐྱར་འདེབས་ཀྱི་ལས་འགུལ་ཅི་ཆེ་བྱེད་བཞིན་ཡང་། ཞིང་ནགས་སྐྱོར་བཙོམ་གྱི་ལས་ཤུགས་དེ་ཞིང་ནགས་བསྐྱར་འདེབས་ལས་འགུལ་ལས་ལྡབས་བཅུ་སྐོར་གྱིས་ལྷག་པ་ཡོད་རེད། བསྐྱར་འདེབས་བྱེད་པའི་ཞིང་རིགས་ཀྱང་ཕལ་ཆེ་བ་ཁེ་ཚོང་སོགས་ལ་དམིགས་པ་མ་གཏོགས་སྐྱོག་ཆགས་ཀྱི་བརྟེ་གནས་སུ་རུང་བའི་ཞིང་ནགས་བསྐྱར་གསོ་བྱུང་བ་ཧ་ཅང་ཉུང་ངུ་རེད། རགས་རྩིས་ལྟར་ན། ལོ་རེ་བཞིན་ཚ་དྲོད་ཆེ་སར་གྱི་བའི་ཞིང་རིགས་རྒྱ་ཁྱོན་སེག་ཟུར་ས་ཡ་ ༡༢ སོར་རྩ་བརྡུག་ཏུ་འགྲོ་བཞིན་རེད། །

༢ འཁོར་ཡུག་གི་གནས་སྟངས་ལེགས་བཅོས་ཆེད་ཡར་རྒྱས་ཀྱི་ལས་ཐབས།

ཡར་རྒྱས་ལས་ཐབས་རྒྱ་ཆེ་ཁག་མང་ལག་བསྟར་བྱས་ཡོད་ཅིང་། དེ་དག་བསྡུས་ན། སྒྲིག་འཛུགས་དང་། དམིགས་བསལ་ཐབས་བྱུས། དཔལ་འབྱོར་གྱི་ལས་ཐབས་བཅས་རེད།

སྒྲིག་འཛུགས་ཀྱི་ཡར་རྒྱས་ལས་ཐབས།

༡༩༧༢ ལོར་གཞུང་གི་སྒྲིག་འཛུགས་ཁོངས་འཁོར་ཡུག་སྲུང་སྐྱོབ་ཆེད་བློན་ཆེན་ལྷན་ཁང་ངམ་ལས་ཁུངས་མ་ལག་ཟུར་དུ་ཡོད་པའི་རྒྱལ་ཁབ་བཅུ་གྲངས་ལས་མེད་ཀྱང་། ད་ཆ་དེ་འདྲའི་སྒྲིག་འཛུགས་ཡོད་པའི་རྒྱལ་ཁབ་བཅུ་འགྱུར་གྱིས་གྲངས་འཕར་ཕྱིན་ཡོད་རེད། འདི་ནི་འཁོར་ཡུག་གི་གནས་དོན་ཐོག་གཞུང་ཐོག་ནས་དོ་སྣང་བྱེད་ཀྱི་ཡོད་པའི་རྟགས་པ་ཞིག་རེད། ལྷག་པར་འདས་མ་ཐག་པའི་ལོ་ངོ་བཅུ་ཕྲག་ཕྱེད་གཉིས་རིང་རྒྱལ་ཁབ་ཕལ་ཆེ་བས་འཁོར་ཡུག་སྲུང་སྐྱོབ་ཆེད་ཁྲིམས་ལུགས་ཡོད་བཞིན་ལ་བསྐྱར་ཞིབ་དང་ སྔར་མེད་ཁྲིམས་ལུགས་གསར་གཏོད་བྱས་པ་སོགས་བྱུང་ཡོད་རེད། ལས་འགུལ་འདི་རིགས་མངའ་སྡེ་དང་ས་གནས་སོ་སོར་ཡང་སྲོལ་གཏོད་ལག་བསྟར་བྱེད་བཞིན་རེད།

རྒྱལ་སྤྱིའི་ཐད་ནས་བྱས་ནའང་། ད་ཆ་འཁོར་ཡུག་ཚོད་བཙུད་སྲུང་སྐྱོབ་ཆེད་དང་རང་བྱུང་ཐོན་རྫས་རྣམས་ལ་རྒྱ་མཚན་ལྡན་པས་ཡོངས་སྤྱོད་བྱ་ཐུས་བཅས་ཀྱི་ཆེད་རྒྱལ་སྤྱིའི་ཆིངས་ཡིག་གྲོས་མཐུན་ཁག་ ༤༠ ཙམ་ཡོད་རེད།

ཕྱི་ཁམས་འཁོར་ཡུག་ཐོག་ཤེས་ཡོན་སློབ་སྦྱོང་དང་དོན་གཉེར།

འཁོར་ཡུག་གི་གནས་དོན་སྐོར་གལ་ཆེར་ངོས་འཛིན་བྱས་ཏེ་སློབ་གྲྭ་དང་མཐོ་སློབ་ཁག་ཕལ་ཆེ་བར་འདི་སྐོར་སློབ་ཚན་དམིགས་བསལ་ཟུར་འཛུགས་བྱས་ཡོད། རྒྱལ་སྤྱིའི་ཉམས་ཞིབ་ཚིག་ཐོ་ཞིག་ལྟར་ན། ཉུང་མཐར་ཡང་སློབ་གཉེར་ཁང་ ༢༩༨ ནས་འཁོར་ཡུག་དང་འབྲེལ་ཡོད་སློབ་ཚན་སྣ་ཚོགས་ཐོག་དམིགས་བསལ་སློབ་སྦྱོང་

སྒྲིད་ཐོན་བྱེད་བཞིན་རེད་ཅེས་བཀོད་ཡོད།

གནས་ཚུལ་གསལ་བསྒྲགས་ཀྱི་ཐབས་ལམ་རྣམས་ལ་བརྟེན་ནས་འཁོར་ཡུག་གི་གནས་སྟངས་སྐོར་སྤྱི་ཡོངས་ངོ་སྣང་དང་དོན་གཉེར་ཆེ་རུ་ཕྱིན་ཡོད། ཚགས་ཤོག་ཕལ་ཆེ་བའི་ནང་འཁོར་ཡུག་སྐོར་དམིགས་བསལ་རྩོམ་བྲིས་ཐེལ་འདོན་བྱེད་ཀྱི་ཡོད་རེད། འཁོར་ཡུག་གི་རྐྱེན་ངན་གནས་ཚུལ། དཔེར་ན། རྒྱ་གར་གྱི་བོ་པལ་གྲོང་ཁྱེར་དང་། རུ་སུའི་ཅར་ནོ་བལ། ལུད་སིའི་གཙང་པོ་ར་ཡིན་བཅས་ལ་བྱུང་བའི་རྐྱེན་ངན་གནས་ཚུལ་རྣམས་ཁྱབ་གྲགས་ཤ་ཚང་ཆེན་པོ་ཕྱིན་ཡོད་རེད། འཁོར་ཡུག་ཐོག་དོན་གཉེར་ཆེ་རུ་ཕྱིན་པ་ལ་བརྟེན་ནས་མང་ཤ། །ཚོགས་ཁྲོད་དུ་སྲུང་སྐྱོབ་ཀྱི་ལས་འགུལ་ཆེ་ཕྲ་མང་པོ་གསར་གཏོད་ཡོད་བཞིན་རེད།

དམིགས་བསལ་ཐབས་བྱུས་ཁག།

འཁོར་ཡུག་བཙོག་སྐྱོན་ཀྱི་ཉེས་སྐྱོན་རྣམས་སེལ་འགོག་སླད་དམིགས་བསལ་འཕྲུལ་ལས་ཀྱི་ཐབས་བྱུས་ཤིན་ཏུ་མང་པོ་ཡོད། ལས་འགུལ་འདི་རིགས་ཐོག་མར་འཕྲུལ་ལས་ཡར་རྒྱས་ཟིན་པའི་རྒྱལ་ཁབ་ཁག་ཏུ་ལག་ལེན་བྱུང་སྟེ། ལས་འགུལ་དེ་དཀ་ཐོག་ད་ཚ་འགྲོ་གྲོན་པོ་རེ་ནས་འཕར་སྟོན་བྱེད་བཞིན་རེད།

དཔལ་འབྱོར་གྱི་ལས་ཐབས།

འཁོར་ཡུག་བདག་སྐྱོང་དང་ཉེས་སྐྱོན་རིགས་འགོག་སླད་དཔལ་འབྱོར་གྱི་ལས་ཐབས་མང་པོ་ཡང་ལག་བསྟར་བྱེད་བཞིན་རེད། ལས་ཐབས་འདི་དག་ནི། འཁོར་ཡུག་ལ་བཙོག་སྐྱོན་སོགས་ཉེས་སྐྱོན་ཡོང་གཞིའི་ལས་ཁག་ལ་དམིགས་བསལ་ཁྲལ་འགེལ་བྱེད་པ་དང་འཁོར་ཡུག་ཡར་རྒྱས་ལས་འགུལ་འབྲེལ་ཡོད་བཅས་ལ་དཔལ་འབྱོར་གྱི་ཆ་ཡངས་གཏོང་བ་སོགས་རེད།

༣ མ་འོངས་པར་དགོས་མཁོའི་གནས།

མི་འབོར་གྲངས་འཕེལ་འགྲོ་བ་དང་མཉམ་དུ་མི་ཚེའི་གནས་སྟངས་ཡར་རྒྱས་ལ་དོན་གཉེར་ཅན་གྱི་མི་གྲངས་ཀྱང་འཕེལ་ངེས་ཡིན་པ་དང་། དེ་ལ་བརྟེན་ནས་རང་བྱུང་ཐོན་ཟོག་ཁག་དང་འཁོར་ཡུག་འདོད་ཡོན་ལོངས་སྤྱོད་ལའང་ཕན་གནོད་དངོས་སུ་འབྲེལ་བ་ཞིག་རེད། དེར་བརྟེན་མ་འོངས་ཐོན་མཐོང་གི་ཐབས་བྱུས་གང་འདྲ་ཞིག་ལ་བརྟེན་ནས་སྐབས་སོ་སོའི་མིའི་འདོད་པ་ཁེངས་པ་དང་སྣོད་ཀྱི་འཁོར་ཡུག་ལ་ཚབས་ཆེའི་གནོད་སྐྱོན་མི་འབྱུང་ཞིག་བྱ་དགོས་པར་བསམ་ཞིབ་བྱ་རྒྱུ་གལ་ཆེན་པོ་རེད།

འདི་ཐད་དུ་ཆ་རྫར་ཡོད་འཚོ་གནས་ཐུབ་ཐོག་ནས་ཡར་རྒྱས་ལས་འགུལ་བརྩམ་ཐབ་ས་ཞིག་བྱུང་ན་ཧ་ཀོང་གི་ཉེན་འགན་ལ་གཏོང་ཞེན་ཐུབ་པར་ངེས་འཛིན་བྱེད་ཀྱི་ཡོད་རེད། གཞི་རྩའི་དམིགས་ཡུལ་འདི་འགྲུབ་ཆེད་གཤམ་གསལ་ཐབས་ཚུལ་ཁག་ལ་ལག་ལེན་བསྟར་དགོས།

༧། སྲིག་འཛུགས་ཕྲ་ཚོགས།

འཁོར་ཡུག་སྲུང་སྐྱོབ་དང་ཡར་རྒྱས་ཆེད་དམིགས་བསལ་གཞུང་གི་སྲིག་འཛུགས་ཇི་ཡོད་རྣམས་ཡར་རྒྱས་ཕྲ་ཚོགས་བྱ་རྒྱུ་གལ་ཆེན་པོ་རེད། དེ་དག་ལ་ཡར་རྒྱས་ལས་འཁྱོལ་རིགས་རྩོམ་སྒྲིག་འཆར་གཞི་འགོད་སྒྲིག་དང་འཕྲོ་གྲོན་ཇི་དགོས་བཅས་ཀྱི་མཐུན་རྐྱེན་སྦྱར་རྒྱུ་དེ་བས་ཀྱང་ཆེན་པོ་རེད།

འཁོར་ཡུག་ལ་བདག་སྐྱོང་རྩིས་བཤེར།

རྒྱལ་ཁབ་ཀྱི་དཔལ་འབྱོར་ནོར་ཡོན་ལ་བདག་སྐྱོང་དང་རྩིས་བཤེར་བྱེད་པ་བཞིན་དུ། འཁོར་ཡུག་གི་ཆུ་རླུང་ཞིང་ས་སོགས་ཀྱི་སྣུས་ཚད་དང་ལེགས་བཅོས་སོགས་ལ་ཡང་བདག་སྐྱོང་དང་རྩིས་བཤེར་བྱ་རྒྱུ་དང་། དེ་དག་གི་ཆེད་དུ་འཕྲོ་གྲོན་སོགས་ཐབ་ཆ་ཟུར་འཛུགས་བྱུང་ན་དགེ་མཚན་ཆེན་པོ་ཡོང་གི་རེད།

སྤེལ་པའི་ནོར་སྐྱོངས།

འཁོར་ཡུག་སྲུང་སྐྱོབ་ཆེད་ཉེས་སྐྱོན་སྟངས་འཛིན་ཁོ་ན་ལྟ་བུ་མ་ཡིན་པར། ཉེས་སྐྱོན་འགོག་ཐབས་དང་། ཕྱག་པར་ཟོན་འགོག་བྱ་ཚུལ་སོགས་གནས་ཚུལ་ཡོངས་རྫོགས་ལ་སློབ་སྦྱོང་དང་ལྡན་པའི་གོ་ནས་ལས་འཁྱོལ་རིགས་རྩོམ་དགོས་ཤིང་། དེ་འདྲ་འབྱུང་བར་ཐོག་མར་གནས་ཚུལ་དེ་དག་སྤེལ་ཚང་གི་ནོར་སྐྱོང་བྱ་རྒྱུ་གལ་ཆེར་ངོས་འཛིན་བྱེད་བཞིན་རེད།

ལག་ལེན་དང་སྨྲ་བརྗོད།

འཁོར་ཡུག་སྲུང་སྐྱོབ་དང་ཡར་རྒྱས་ཆེད་ཁྲིམས་ལུགས་ཇི་ཡོད་རྣམས་ལག་ལེན་དོན་འཁེལ་ཡོང་སྒྲིག་འཆར་གཞི་དང་དཔལ་འབྱོར་སོགས་གང་ས་ནས་མཐུན་རྐྱེན་སྦྱར་ཏེ་ལག་ལེན་ཁེལ་ཐབས་བྱ་དགོས། འདི་དག་ཐོག་དམིགས་བསལ་གྱི་སྨྲ་བརྗོད་རིགས་སྤྲད་ཐུབ་ན་ཕན་ཐོགས་ཡོང་གི་རེད།

ཐབས་ཚུལ་ཁྱབ་བསྒྲགས།

འཁོར་ཡུག་གི་གང་ཅིའི་གནས་དོན་རྣམས་མང་ཚོགས་ལ་ཁྱབ་བསྒྲགས་ཐུབ་པ་གལ་ཆེན་རེད།

ཡ་རབས་བཟང་སྤྱོད་ཀྱི་ཡར་རྒྱས།

ལས་དོན་ཇི་འདྲ་ཞིག་ཡིན་རུང་གྲུབ་འབྲས་ལེགས་པོ་ཐོན་པར་མཐར་ཐུག་གི་རྐྱེན་རྩའི་ཐོག་ཏུ་ཤུགས་སྤེལ་དགོས་ཕལ་ཆེར་གྱིས་འདོད་ཀྱི་ཡོད་པ་ལྟར། འཁོར་ཡུག་གི་སྣུས་ཚད་དང་རང་བྱུང་ཐོན་ཟས་རྣམས་ཀྱི་ལོངས་སྤྱོད་བྱ་ཚུལ་བཅས་ཀྱང་མཐར་གཏུགས་ན། མི་བྱེ་བྲག་སོ་སོའི་གང་ཅིའི་སྤྱོད་ཚུལ་འཕྱུར་སྟངས་དང་ལག་ལེན་བཅས་ལ་རག་ལུས་ཡ་ཞིག་རེད། མི་བྱེ་བྲག་མང་པོའི་སྤྱོད་ཚུལ་གཞན་ལ་དཔེ་སྟོན་ཐུབ་པའི་རིགས་བྱུང་ན། སྤྱི་ཡོངས་ལ་ཕན་གནོད་ཆེན་པོ་འབྲེལ་གྱི་རེད། དེར་བརྟེན་མི་སེར་རེ་རེ་ནས་ཀུན་སློང་དང་

སྤྱོད་ཚུལ་བཅོས་ཏེ་ཡར་རབས་བཟང་སྤྱོད་ལ་བསྐུལ་ཐུབ་ན་རང་ལུགས་ཀྱིས་ཕན་ཐོགས་ཆེན་པོ་འབྱུང་ངེས་རེད། སྲོག་ཆགས་གཞན་ལ་སྙིང་བརྩེ་དང་བཟོད་བསྲན་བྱེད་པ། སྲོག་ཟན་ཡོངས་ལ་བརྩེ་སྲུང་བྱེད་པ། རང་བྱུང་འཁོར་ཡུག་ལ་དབང་བསྒྱུར་བྱ་འདོད་ཀྱི་བསམ་བློ་དོར་ཏེ། དེ་དག་གི་ཁམས་གཉིས་དང་མཐུན་པར་སྤྱོད་པ། རང་བྱུང་ཐོན་རྫས་རྣམས་དང་འཁོར་ཡུག་གི་འདོད་ཡོན་རྣམས་ད་ལྟ་དང་མ་འོངས་པའི་མི་རབས་གཉིས་ཀའི་ཐུན་མོང་གི་མཁོ་ཕན་ཆེད་སྤྱོད་པ། དགོས་མེད་ཀྱི་སྤྱོད་ཟད་མི་བྱེད་པ་བཅས་ནི་གཞི་རྩའི་སྤྱོད་ཚུལ་དང་ལག་ལེན་ཁྲོད་འཕེལ་གཏོང་དགོས་རྣམས་རེད།

སྟོན་པ་ཤཱཀྱ་ཐུབ་པས་ལོ་ཉིས་སྟོང་བརྒལ་བའི་སྔོན་དུ་ཡ་རབས་ཀྱི་སྤྱོད་ཚུལ་འདི་དག་གཞན་ལ་བསྟན་པ་དང་རང་གིས་ཉམས་བཞེས་གནང་ཡོད་རེད། སྤྱོད་ཚུལ་འདི་དག་ནི་དེང་སང་ཡང་ཉམས་ལེན་བྱ་འོས་ཅིག་ཏུ་མ་ཟད། ལྷག་པར་ཡང་ཕན་འབྲེལ་ཆེན་པོར་གྱུར་ཡོད་རེད།

ད་ལྟ་དང་མ་འོངས་པར་དགོས་མཁོ་ཞེས་པའི་རྩོམ་ཡིག་འདི་ནི། ཀྱི་ཕོ་ཞིར་རེ་རེ་ནས་འཁོར་ཡུག་གི་གཞི་རྩའི་གནས་ཚུལ་གལ་ཆེ་རྣམས་ལ་དོན་གཉེར་དང་འབྲེལ། དེ་དང་འབྲེལ་བའི་ཡ་རབས་ཀྱི་སྤྱོད་ཚུལ་དང་ལག་ལེན་ཐུབ་པའི་ཆེད་དུ་བརྩམས་པ་ཡིན།། །།

·····ཕྱི་ཁམས་འཁོར་ཡུག་གི་གང་ཅིའི་གནས་ཚུལ་སྐོར་ལ་མཁས་དབང་ཉག་ཙར་ནེ་ས་ཀུན་ནས་བརྩམས་པའི་སྐོར་གསལ་རྩོམ་བྲིས་དབྱིན་སྐད་ཐོག་ནས་བརྗོད་དོན་སྙིང་བསྡུས་ཤིག་བོད་སྐད་དུ་ཕབ་བསྒྱུར་བྱས་པ་དང་། རྒྱས་ཞིབ་ཕབ་བསྒྱུར་ཡང་བྱེད་བཞིན་ཡིན་པ་བཅས།། །།

༄༅། ནང་ཆོས་ཕྱོགས་ནས་རང་བྱུང་ཁམས་ལ་ཧྲ་ཕྱོགས་ཀྱི་ལས་འགུལ།

ནན་སི་ནེ་བི།

༄༅། ནང་ཆོས་ཕྱོགས་ནས་རང་བྱུང་ཁམས་ལ་ཧྲ་ཕྱོགས་ཀྱི་ལས་འགུལ་འདི་ནི་ནང་པ་ནང་ཁུལ་གྱི་རང་བྱུང་ཁམས་ཕྱོགས་ཧྲ་ཚོལ་དང༌། ཧྲ་སྲུང་ལེགས་སུ་གཏོང་རྒྱའི་སློབ་གསོའི་ལས་འགུལ་ཞིག་ཡིན་ལ་འཛམ་གླིང་མི་མང་ཡོངས་ནས་ཡ་རབས་སྤྱོད་བཟང་གི་ཕྱོགས་ནས་རང་བྱུང༌། ཁམས་སྲུང་སྐྱོབ་བྱེད་རྒྱུར་དོ་སྣང་ཡོང་བའི་ཆེད་དུ་ཡང་ཡིན།

ཉེ་བའི་ལོ་བཅུ་ཕྲུག་འགའ་ཤས་ནང་མིའི་ཤེས་བྱ་རིག་པ་དང༌། ཚན་རིག་གི་གསར་གཏོད་གྲུབ་འབྲས་ནི་ཧ་ལས་དགོས་པ་ཞིག་བྱུང་ཡོད་པ་རེད། ཡིན་ནའང་ང་ཚོས་ངོ་མཚར་ཀྱི་བའི་གྲུབ་འབྲས་དེ་དག་དང་མཉམ་པའམ། ཡང་ན་དེ་ལས་ཉུག་པའི་རང་བྱུང་ཁམས་ལ་གཏོར་བཤིག་གི་ཉམས་ཆགས་ཆེན་པོ་བྱུང་ཡོད་པ་རེད། གཏོར་བཤིག་དེ་དག་ནི་དུས་ཚོད་ཐུང་ངུའི་ནང་གཞི་རྒྱ་ཆེན་པོ་ཞིག་བཏང་བའི་རྐྱེན་གྱིས་སོ་ནམ་དང་འཕྲོད་བསྟེན་སོགས་ལ་དམིགས་བསལ་གྱི་དོ་སྣང་བྱེད་རྒྱུར་འགོག་རྐྱེན་མང་པོ་ཞིག་བཟོས་ཡོད་པ་རེད།

རང་བྱུང་ཁམས་སྲུང་སྐྱོབ་བྱེད་རྒྱུ་དེ་ནི་གཞུང་དང༌། སེར་གྱི་ཚོགས་པ་ཁག་གི་རྩེ་འཁྲིད་པའི་ལས་འགུལ་ཞིག་ཡིན་པ་དང༌། དེ་ནི་འགྲོ་བ་མིའི་ལོ་རྒྱུས་ནང་ཉེ་བའི་ཆར་བྱུང་བའི་འགྱུར་བ་གསར་པ་ཞིག་ཀྱང་རེད། ལོ་བཅུ་ཕྲུག་འགའ་ཞིག་ཕྱིན་པའི་ལས་འགུལ་འདི་ནི་རྒྱལ་སྤྱིའི་ནང་གནད་འགག་ཆེ་བའི་ལས་འགུལ་ཞིག་ཡིན་ལ་ད་དུང་ངོས་འཛིན་དང་ཁྱབ་བདལ་རྒྱ་ཆེར་འགྲོ་ཐུབ་རེད།

ཕྱིར་འཛམ་གླིང་འདིའི་རྫོང་བཅད་ཉམས་ཆགས་མི་འགྲོ་བའི་ཐབས་ལམ་དམིགས་བསལ་ཁ་གསལ་པ་ཞིག་མེད་ནའང་ང་ཚོས་རྟོགས་པའི་འཛམ་གླིང་འདི་བཞིན་དུ་མུར་རྒྱུན་རིང་གནས་ཐུབ་པའི་ཐབས་ཤེས་ཀྱི་སློབ་སྦྱོང་མང་པོ་ཞིག་བྱེད་རྒྱུ་དེ་ནི་གལ་ཆེ་ཤོས་ཤིག་ཆགས་ཡོད་པ་རེད། ད་ཡོད་རང་བྱུང་ཁམས་དང༌། རང་བྱུང་གནས་ཀྱི་སྲུང་སྐྱོབ་བྱེད་རྒྱུའི་སློབ་གསོ་མང་ཆེ་བ་ནི་ང་ཚོར་ཐྲལ་སེལ་དཀའ་ངལ་འཕྲད་པའི་སྐབས་ཀྱི་ཐབས་ལམ་ཤ་སྟག་རེད། ད་ཆ་ཚན་རིག་གི་ཕྱོགས་ནས་ཐོན་སྐྱེད་དང༌། ཕྱུག་ཆགས་ཀྱི་དཀའ་ངལ། བཟོ་བསྐྲུན་གྱི་དཀའ་ངལ་སོགས་དེ་དག་རྒྱུན་འཁྱོངས་ནས་སེལ་ཐབས་སུ་ཤུགས་རྩོན་སྐྱུག་གི་ཡོད་པ་རེད།

རང་བྱུང་ཁོར་ཡུག་གི་སྲུང་སྐྱོབ་ལ་ཚན་རིག་གི་ལས་ཀ་ནི་མེད་དུ་མི་རུང་བ་ཞིག་རེད། ཚན་རིག་ཕྱོགས་ནས་བརྟག་དཔྱད་ཞིབ་འཇུག་བྱས་རྗེས་གལ་གནད་ཆེ་ཆུང་དབྱེ་འབྱེད་ཀྱིས་འཛམ་གླིང་གི་འགོ་འཁྲིད་དང༌། འཆར་གཞི་ཐག་གཅོད་བྱེད་མཁན་རྣམས་ལ་འབོད་བསྐུལ་གྱིས་རང་བྱུང་ཁམས་ལ་སྲུང་

སྐྱོབ་ཐུབ་པ་དགོས་རྒྱུ། དཔེར་ན་མིའི་མ་རིག་པ་དང་། འདོད་རྔམས། ཁོར་ཡུག་ལ་བཅོས་ཞེན་མེད་པའི་མི་ཡི་བྱ་སྤྱོད་ཀྱི་རྐྱེན་གྱིས་ས་རྡུལ་བརྒྱབ་པ་དང་། ཆུ་རློགས་མ་ཆགས་པ་སོགས་ཀྱི་དཀའ་ངལ་བྱུང་བ་ཞིག་རེད།

ནང་ཆོས་ནས་རང་བྱུང་ཁམས་ལ་ཧ་ཕྱོགས་ཀྱི་ལས་འགུལ་དེའི་ནང་ཚན་རིག་གཙོ་བོར་འཛིན་རྒྱུ་ཡིན། དེང་འཛམ་གླིང་ནང་མི་འབོར་ཇེ་ཆེར་འཕེལ་རྒྱས་འགྲོ་བཞིན་པ་དང་། མིའི་རེ་འདུན། དགོས་མཁོ་ཇེ་མང་དུ་ཕྱིན་པའི་སྐབས་དེར་འཛམ་གླིང་སྟོད་ཀྱི་བཟོ་མི་ཐུབ་པའི་ཁུངས་རྒྱུ་མས་ཆེས་ཉུང་དུ་ཕྱིན་ཡོད་པ་རེད།

ལས་འགུལ་འདི་བཞིན་ཤེས་ཡོན་གྱི་ཐོག་ནས་ཧ་ཕྱོགས་གསར་པ་ཞིག་ཡིན་པ་མ་ཟད། འདིའི་ནང་འགྲོ་བ་མིའི་རིག་གཞུང་དང་། སྐྱེ་ཚོགས་ཀྱི་གནས་སྟངས། འདུ་ཤེས་འཛིན་སྟངས། འདུ་ཤེས་འཛིན་སྟངས་སོགས་ལ་ལྷག་གལ་ཆེར་བཅིས་ཏེ་རྩ་འཛིན་བྱེད་ཀྱི་ཡོད་པ་རེད། དེ་ཡང་དཀའ་ངལ་སེལ་ཐབས་པའི་གལ་ཆེའི་ནུས་པ་ཡོད་པའི་ཤེས་ཡོན་གྱི་བསླབ་བྱ་དེ་ཚོར་དེ་ཙམ་གྱི་དོ་སྣང་མ་བྱེད་པར་སྣང་ཚང་བྱུང་ཡོད་པ་རེད།

ནང་ཆོས་ཐོག་ནས་རང་བྱུང་ཁམས་ལ་ཧ་ཕྱོགས་ཀྱི་ལས་འགུལ་འདིའི་ནང་ཐོག་མར་ཁྱིམ་ཚང་ཞིག་ནས་འགོ་ཚུགས་ཀྱི་དངོས་གཞིའི་སློབ་གསོ་དང་། འགོ་འཁྲིད་ཀྱི་འགན་དབང་བར་ཤེས་ཡོན་གྱི་ངོ་བོ་ཆ་ཚང་བ་ཞིག་ཡོད། ཁྱིམ་ཚང་རེ་རེ་དང་། གྲོང་སྡེ་སོ་སོའི་ནང་ཐུན་མོང་མ་ཡིན་པའི་ཁྱད་ཆོས་རིག་གཞུང་དང་། ཡ་རབས་ཀུན་སྤྱོད་ཀྱི་ཐོག་ནས་ཤེས་ཡོན་ཐེབ་ཐུབ་ཀྱི་ཡོད་པ་རེད། ཤེས་ཡོན་དེའི་ནང་ལོ་ ༣༥༠༠ ཙག་ཙམ་རྗེན་གྱི་ནང་པའི་ཕྱག་དཔེ་དང་། རྗེབས་རིས་སོགས་ནས་རང་བྱུང་ཁམས་སྲུང་སྐྱོབ་དགོས་པའི་སློབ་གསོ་རྣམས་བརྡ་རྟུབ་ཀྱི་དེབ་ཆུང་དང་། གློག་བརྙན་སོགས་ནས་དེང་དུས་ཤེས་ཡོན་སྤྲོད་སྟངས་ཀྱི་ལམ་ནས་སྐྱེ་ཚོགས་ནང་སློབ་གསོ་སྤྲོད་ཐུབ་ཀྱི་ཡོད་པ་རེད།

ཕྱི་ལོ་ ༡༩༨༥ ལོར་འགོ་བཙུགས་པའི་ཉམས་ཞིབ་ལས་འགུལ་འདི་ནི་བོད་གཞུང་ཆོས་རིག་ཞབས་ཁང་དང་། བོད་གཞུང་དྲིལ་བསྒྲགས་ཞབས་ཁང་གཉིས་ནས་ཐོག་པ་ཆེན་པོའི་གཞུང་ནས་ཉམས་ཞིབ་གནང་རྒྱུ་དང་། ཝྜ་ཡི་ལེན་ཊེ་རི་དྭགས་ཚོགས་པ་དང་། ཝྜ་ཡི་གཞུང་གི་ཤེས་རིག་ཞབས་ཁང་། ཐ་མ་ས་མཛོ་སློབ་བཅས་ནས་ཐེག་དམན་གྱི་གཞུང་ལུགས་ནས་ཉམས་ཞིབ་ཀྱིས་འགོ་ཚུགས་བྱེད་རྒྱུ་ཡིན། ཐོག་མར་བོད་དང་ཝྜ་ཡི་ཝེན་ཊེའི་ནང་པ་ནས་འགོ་བཙུགས་པའི་ལས་འགུལ་ཞིག་ཡིན་ནའང་ལས་དོན་ཉམས་ཞིབ་བྱས་པའི་སྐབས་ནང་པའི་རྒྱལ་ཁབ་གཞན་དང་། ཕྱི་ཚོགས་ཁག་ལ་འབྲེལ་བ་རྒྱ་ཆེ་བྱུང་ཡོད། པ་དེ་ནི་དཀའ་བསྡུའི་རང་བཞིན་ཡིན་པ་དང་། ལས་འགུལ་འདི་ནི་ནང་པའི་གཞུང་དང་། ཚོགས་པ། སྒེར་པ་སུ་རུང་གི་བེད་སྤྱོད་བྱེད་འདོད་ཡོད་པ་རྣམས་ལ་སློབ་གསོའི་ཡིག་ཆ་དང་། དཔར་

དེབ་སོགས་སྤྲོད་རྒྱུའི་དམིགས་ཡུལ་ཡོད་པ་རེད།

ཤེས་ཡོན་སློབ་སྦྱོང་སྤྲོད་སྟངས་གསར་པའི་འདིར་ནང་པའི་ཆོས་དེ་བཞིན་ཆུ་ཚོད་ཀྱི་ཆེད་དུ་འདེམས་སྒྲུག་བྱས་པ་ཞིག་ཡོད་ན། ནང་ཆོས་གཞུང་ལུགས་ཀྱི་བསླབ་བྱ་རྣམས་ཡུན་རིང་རྒྱུན་བརྟན་གནས་པའི་རིག་པའི་གཞུང་ཞིག་ཡིན་པ་དང་། སེམས་ཅན་ཐམས་ཅད་ཡིད་ལ་དྲན་ཏེ་བྱམས་སྙིང་རྗེ་བྱེད་དགོས་པའི་བསླབ་བྱ་ཡོད་པ་རེད། དེ་བཞིན་ཨོ་མི་ཡའི་གླིང་ཆེན་ས་ཁུལ་མང་པོའི་ནང་ཐུན་མོང་མ་ཡིན་པའི་རིག་དངོས་རིགས་མང་པོ་ཞིག་རྩ་སྒྲོངས་འགྱོ་ཉེན་ཡོད་པར་བརྟེན་ནང་པའི་བསླབ་བྱ་དེ་དག་ཕན་ནུས་ཆེ་ལ་གཞི་རྒྱ་ཆེ་བར་ཁྱབ་ཐུབ་ཀྱི་ཡོད་པ་རེད། དེ་བཞིན་ཨོ་མི་ཡའི་ཕྱོང་གསེབ་ས་ཁུལ་མང་པོའི་ནང་སློབ་སྦྱོང་བྱེད་རྒྱུར་ནང་པའི་ཆོས་ཀྱི་བསླབ་བྱ་དེ་གཙོ་བོ་ཡིན་ཞབས་ནང་པའི་ཆོས་ཀྱི་ཐོག་ནས་རྩ་སྒྲོངས་འགྱོ་ཉེན་གྱི་སྐད་ཆགས་ཀྱི་རིགས་དེ་དག་སྲུང་སྐྱོབ་བྱ་རྒྱུར་ཕན་ནུས་ཤུགས་ཆེ་ཡོད་པ་རེད།

འཛམ་གླིང་རྒྱལ་ཁབ་གང་སར་རང་བྱུང་ཁམས་སྲུང་སྐྱོབ་བྱེད་རྒྱུར་དོ་སྣང་ཤུགས་ཆེ་ཡོད་པར་བརྟེན་ནང་ཆོས་ཐོག་ནས་ལས་འགུལ་ཐེལ་བཏོད་དང་། ཆོས་ལུགས་གཞན་ཁག་རྣམས་དང་འབྲེལ་གཏུག་ཀྱིས་འཆར་གཞི་གསར་བཟོ་ཐུབ་རྒྱུར་ཡང་ཕན་ཐོགས་ཆེན་པོ་ཡོད་པ་ཞིག་རེད།

ནང་ཆོས་ཐོག་ནས་རང་བྱུང་ཁམས་ལ་ལྟ་ཕྱོགས་ཀྱི་ལས་འགུལ་འདི་བཞིན་རྒྱལ་སྤྱིའི་གལ་གནད་ཆེ་བའི་ཚོགས་པ་ཁག་དང་། གེར་པ་མང་པོས་རྒྱབ་སྐྱོར་གནང་བ་རྣམས་ལ་ང་ཚོས་སྙིང་ཐག་པ་ནས་ཐུགས་རྗེ་ཆེ་ཞུ་རྒྱུ་དང་། དགའ་བསུའི་ངང་གཏམ་དུ་མཚོན་གཞུང་བཀོད་རྒྱུ་ཡིན།

རྩམ་ཀུ་ནན་སི་ནེ་མི་མཆོག་ནང་ཆོས་ཐོག་ནས་རང་བྱུང་ཁམས་ལ་ལྟ་ཕྱོགས་ཀྱི་ལས་འགུལ་འབུ་འཛུགས་མཁན་དང་། དེའི་སྐོར་རྒྱལ་སྤྱིའི་ནང་འཕོ་འཕྲིད་མཁན་ཡིན། ཁོང་ནས་ད་བར་སྟོག་ཆགས་དང་རང་བྱུང་ཁམས་སྲུང་སྐྱོང་སྐོར་རྩོམ་ཡིག་ཁག ༣༠ སྐུག་གནང་ཡོད། རྒྱ་ནག་རྒྱལ་སྤྱིའི་རིག་དངོས་ཚོགས་པ་གསར་འཛུགས་ཀྱི་འབྲེལ་ལམ་འཆར་འདོན་ཡང་ཁོང་ནས་གནང་ཡོད་པ་རེད།།

The Rolex Awards for Enterprise

พระพุทธศาสนาเพื่อธรรมชาติ ได้รับรางวัล โรเล็กซ์ ประจำปี 2530 ประเภท สิ่งแวดล้อม

ต้นไม้แห่งชีวิต

พระพุทธศาสนากับการอนุรักษ์ธรรมชาติ

บทนำ

โดย เซอร์ ปีเตอร์ สก๊อต

โครงการพระพุทธศาสนาเพื่อธรรมชาติ ซึ่งเป็นต้นเค้าของหนังสือเล่มนี้ เป็นแนวโน้มทางการศึกษาแบบใหม่ที่มีความสำคัญในการศึกษาความวิบัติของสิ่งแวดล้อมอันเกิดจากการที่มนุษย์ทำลายธรรมชาติ และวิธีการที่จะนำมาเพื่อการอนุรักษ์ทรัพยากรของโลก

อาจจะดูเป็นเรื่องแปลกที่จะใช้วิธีการศึกษาแบบใหม่โดยใช้คำสอนที่มีมานานกว่า 2,500 ปี แม้ขบวนการอนุรักษ์จะกระทำกันระดับสากล มีองค์กรของรัฐบาลและองค์กรเอกชนเป็นผู้นำมานานกว่าสองทศวรรษแล้วก็ตาม แต่ขบวนการนี้ ก็ยังอยู่ในขั้นเริ่มต้นที่จะเป็นที่ยอมรับโดยทั่วไป เหตุใดจึงพยายามแก้ปัญหาปัจจุบันโดยการใช้คำสอนอันมีมาแต่โบราณกาลเล่า

คำตอบง่ายๆก็คือ แม้ความพยายามในการอนุรักษ์จะเพิ่มขึ้น แต่ก็ไม่อาจจะเทียบได้กับการทำลายล้างสิ่งแวดล้อม ความพยายามที่มีอยู่ในปัจจุบันไม่เพียงพอที่จะรับมือกับปัญหาที่เกิดขึ้นเป็นทวีคูณ

งานอนุรักษ์ธรรมชาติโดยทั่วๆไป จึงมุ่งในการตอบรับวิกฤติการณ์ โดยมุ่งเน้นปัญหาทางชีวภาพ และเสนอสนองวิธีการแก้ไขทางเทคนิค ประสบความสำเร็จในขีดคั่นที่ต่างกันไป แม้กระนั้น การทำลายล้างธรรมชาติและทรัพยากรธรรมชาติก็ยังคงมีอยู่ โดยเป็นปัญหาที่ยังไม่ได้รับความสนใจอย่างแท้จริง

สาเหตุหนึ่ง เป็นด้วยงานอนุรักษ์เป็นงานใหม่....แม้ว่าพวกเราหลายคนอาจจะตระหนักดีว่า เป็นเรื่องน่าเศร้าเพียงใดที่งานนี้เริ่มต้นขึ้นช้ามาก เมื่อพิจารณาถึงความสูญเสียของชีวิต พืชพรรณ และแหล่งที่อยู่ของสัตว์ทั้งหลาย และความจริงที่ว่าขบวนการนี้ถูกจำกัดด้วยกำลังคนและทรัพยากร สาเหตุอีกประการหนึ่ง คือการที่วิกฤติการณ์นั้นๆมักได้รับการเยียวยาช้าเกินการณ์เสมอ

แต่เหตุผลที่สำคัญก็คือ การที่จะต้องเน้นให้เห็นถึงความสำคัญของการอนุรักษ์ในภาคปฏิบัติ บทบาทที่สำคัญของการอนุรักษ์ในด้านเศรษฐกิจ การพัฒนา การเพิ่มผลผลิตทางด้านอาหาร โดยย่ออาจจะกล่าวได้ว่า คือระบบในการคงไว้ซึ่งชีวิตบนพิภพนี้

ความพยายามในการอนุรักษ์จึงมีสาระอย่างยิ่งสำหรับความอยู่ดีกินดีของประชาชนทั้งปัจจุบันและอนาคต แต่ส่วนใหญ่แล้วกลับไม่ได้รับความสนใจ เพราะจุดที่มุ่งเน้นนั้นได้มองข้ามปัจจัยสำคัญทางวัฒนธรรม สังคม และความเชื่อในส่วนบุคคล ในส่วนที่เกี่ยวกับปัญหาของเรา และความสามารถของเราในการแก้ปัญหานั้นๆ

รัฐบาลและผู้นำทางเศรษฐกิจที่มองเห็นการณ์ไกล อาจได้รับการชักชวนให้มีบทบาทยิ่งขึ้นในการอนุรักษ์ธรรมชาติ เพราะความสำคัญของงานที่มีต่อเศรษฐกิจในอนาคต หรือเพื่อเหตุผลทางวิทยาศาสตร์ แต่จะให้ประชาชนปฏิบัติเพียงเพื่อเหตุผลดังกล่าวมิใช่เรื่องง่ายนัก

พวกที่อนุรักษ์หรือทำลายธรรมชาตินั้น กระทำด้วยเหตุผลต่างๆกัน และเหตุผลดังกล่าวนั้น บางอย่างก็ชัดเจน ดังที่องค์ดาไลลามะทรงชี้ให้เห็นในพระราชดำรัสของพระองค์ว่า กิเลสของมนุษย์เป็นปัจจัยสำคัญในการทำลายโลก ปัจจัยนี้กอปรกับการขาดความเคารพในผู้อื่นและชีวิตในรูปแบบอื่น อันมีสาเหตุมาจากสิ่งแวดล้อมทางวัฒนธรรมที่ขาดแคลน

ในหมู่ผู้ที่ทำงานอนุรักษ์อย่างแข็งขันนั้น เราอาจพบนักอนุรักษ์ที่ไม่เคยเข้าป่าเลย แต่มีความรับผิดชอบในการสนับสนุนผู้ที่ทำงานด้านนี้โดยตรง บางครั้งเราพบนักธุรกิจที่ต้องการรักษาผลประโยชน์ของตน บางครั้งเราพบเยาวชนทั่วโลกที่กล่าวด้วยความรู้สึกน่ารักและไร้เดียงสาว่า อยากอนุรักษ์สัตว์เพราะรักสัตว์

นอกจากนี้ก็ยังมีนักวิทยาศาสตร์ ผู้นำในแขนงการศึกษาต่างๆ ที่ให้ความสนับสนุนงานอนุรักษ์ ด้วยเหตุผลหนึ่ง คือ เห็นความสำคัญของพืชพรรณและสัตว์ต่างๆ ข้าพเจ้าได้รู้จักนักวิทยาศาสตร์ นักชีววิทยาสัตว์ป่า และคนอื่นๆ บางคนเป็นผู้ที่มีชื่อเสียงอย่างยิ่งในสายงานอาชีพของเขา และหันมาสนใจงานอนุรักษ์เพราะชื่นชมในความสุนทรีย์ของงานนี้

ด้วยเหตุผลต่างๆ บ่อยครั้งจะมีปัจจัยในด้านแนวความคิดเชิงปรัชญาเข้ามาเกี่ยวข้อง เราพบว่าการศึกษาเป็นปัจจัยสำคัญที่สุดประการหนึ่ง ในการเยียวยาในระยะยาว หากเราจะช่วยให้ชีวิตบนโลกนี้มีอยู่ต่อไป

โครงการพระพุทธศาสนาเพื่อธรรมชาติ และผลงานจากโครงการเช่นหนังสือเล่มนี้ มีความสำคัญต่อวงการอนุรักษ์ทั่วโลก มิได้จำกัดเฉพาะในหมู่ชาวพุทธ แต่อาจจะใช้ได้ทุกจุดในโลกที่ประสบปัญหาเดียวกัน

เราให้การศึกษาในการอนุรักษ์ในทุกระดับ เริ่มต้นจากภายในครอบครัว แล้วแผ่ขยายไปสู่การให้การศึกษาในระบบ และในระดับผู้นำ เรามีรูปแบบที่มีประสิทธิภาพ โดยการให้การศึกษาถึงความสำคัญของการอนุรักษ์ธรรมชาติจากปริบทของวัฒนธรรม โดยเน้นในประเพณี และจริยธรรมซึ่งเป็นที่ยอมรับกันอยู่แล้วในสังคมนั้นๆ

งานทางวิชาการอันน่าประทับใจซึ่งปรากฏในบทความของ ดร.ฉัตรสุมาลย์ กบิลสิงห์ ในเรื่องบทบาทของพระพุทธศาสนากับงานอนุรักษ์ และบทความของ ดร.เนหุน เรื่องสภาวะของสิ่งแวดล้อมในปัจจุบัน เป็นพื้นฐานเนื้อหาของหนังสือเล่มนี้ การอนุรักษ์อันเป็นวิถีชีวิตจะช่วยพัฒนาคุณภาพของชีวิต และคำสอนของพุทธศาสนาในเรื่องความกลมกลืนและการอนุรักษ์สะท้อนให้เห็นถึงนโยบายการบริหารด้านสิ่งแวดล้อมสมัยใหม่มากขึ้น

ข้าพเจ้ามีความยินดีที่ได้ติดตามงานของโครงการพระพุทธศาสนาเพื่อธรรมชาติมาตั้งแต่ต้น ก่อนที่โครงการจะมีชื่อเรียกเช่นนี้เสียด้วยซ้ำ ในพ.ศ.2522 แนนซี่ แนช ผู้ริเริ่มโครงการขณะทำงานเป็นที่ปรึกษาของมูลนิธิคุ้มครองสัตว์ป่าแห่งโลก (World Wildlife Fund) ได้เสนอให้นำศาสนาเข้ามาประยุกต์ในงานอนุรักษ์ นอกจากนี้ เธอยังได้เสนอ

ให้มีการประสานงานระหว่างมูลนิธิฯกับประเทศจีน ทำให้เธอต้องใช้เวลาอยู่กับงานนี้เป็นเวลาหลายปีต่อมา จนได้รับการขนานนามว่า "นางสาวแพนด้า" ต่อมาแนนซี่ได้รับการขอร้องให้ช่วยก่อตั้งองค์การมูลนิธิคุ้มครองสัตว์ป่าแห่งโลกสาขาฮ่องกงอีกด้วย

โครงการในการที่จะนำศาสนาเข้ามาสนับสนุนในงานอนุรักษ์ของเธอ ต้องรออยู่จนกระทั่ง พ.ศ.2528 จึงได้มีการเสนอเค้าโครงและเริ่มงานขึ้น ภายในเวลา 2 ปี โครงการนี้ได้ช่วยทำให้คำสอนของพุทธศาสนาที่เกี่ยวกับความรับผิดชอบของมนุษย์ที่พึงมีต่อธรรมชาติชัดเจนขึ้น และทำให้ประชาชนมรความตื่นตัวยิ่งขึ้นในเรื่องจริยธรรมด้านสิ่งแวดล้อม

พื้นฐานทางจริยธรรมของการอนุรักษ์นั้นเป็นพื้นฐานที่สำคัญยิ่งสำหรับข้าพเจ้าทั้งในชีวิตส่วนตัวและงานที่ทำ ข้าพเจ้าจึงรู้สึกขอบคุณที่ได้เห็นการนำเสนอความคิดนี้ในหนังสือเล่มนี้และในเป้าประสงค์ของโครงการ

องค์ดาไลลามะ ผู้ทรงเป็นชาวพุทธ และทรงเป็นผู้นำทางจิตวิญญาณในระดับนานาชาติได้ประทานพลัง แรงบันดาลใจและความสนับสนุนในงานนี้ตลอดพัฒนาการของโครงการ และเราได้แต่เพียงหวังว่า ผู้นำทางศาสนาท่านอื่นๆ จะดำเนินรอยตามพระราชดำรัสของพระองค์ในด้านจริยธรรมในการอนุรักษ์สิ่งแวดล้อม ดังที่ปรากฏอยู่ในหนังสือเล่มนี้เช่นกัน และหนังสือเล่มนี้ได้รับการตั้งชื่อที่เหมาะสมยิ่งว่า <u>ต้นไม้แห่งชีวิต</u>

เซอร์ ปีเตอร์ สก๊อต CBE, DSC เป็นผู้บุกเบิกงานอนุรักษ์ระดับสากล และเป็นผู้ริเริ่มสหภาพสากลเพื่อการอนุรักษ์ธรรมชาติและแหล่งทรัพยากรธรรมชาติ (IUCN) และมูลนิธิคุ้มครองสัตว์ป่าแห่งโลก (WWF) เป็นผู้บรรยายเรื่องสัตว์ป่า เป็นนักเขียน และเป็นศิลปิน

จริยธรรมในการคุ้มครองสิ่งแวดล้อม

พระราชดำรัสของสมเด็จพระเท็นซิน กยัตโส ดาไลลามะองค์ที่ 14 แห่งธิเบต

ความสงบสุขและความอยู่รอดของชีวิตบนพื้นโลกถูกรุกรานโดยการกระทำของมนุษย์อย่างไร้คุณค่าแห่งมนุษยธรรม

การทำลายธรรมชาติและทรัพยากรทางธรรมชาติเป็นผลของความโง่เขลา ความโลภ และการขาดความเคารพต่อสิ่งมีชีวิตร่วมพิภพ

การขาดความเคารพเช่นนี้ ได้แผ่ขยายลุกลามไปถึงชีวิตของมนุษย์ด้วยกันเอง หากเราไม่สามารถนำสันติสุขมาสู่โลกได้ และการทำลายสภาพทางธรรมชาติยังคงดำเนินไปในอัตราที่เป็นอยู่ มรดกที่อนุชนจะได้รับก็คงจะเหลือเพียงซากของโลกที่ไร้คุณภาพ

บรรพบุรุษของเราได้เห็นโลกที่อุดมสมบูรณ์ ชาวโลกในอดีตเชื่อว่า ธรรมชาติจะคงมีอยู่ต่อไปโดยไม่มีวันหมด แต่เรารู้ว่า ความเชื่อเช่นนั้นจะเป็นจริงก็ต่อเมื่อเราทะนุบำรุงรักษาให้คงสภาพเช่นนั้นต่อไปเท่านั้น

การทำลายธรรมชาติที่ผ่านมาในอดีตนั้น เกิดจากความโง่เขลา จึงให้อภัยได้ไม่ยากนัก แต่ทุกวันนี้ เรามีข้อมูลมากขึ้น จึงจำเป็นอย่างยิ่งที่เราจะต้องตรวจสอบมรดกที่เราได้รับสืบทอดมานี้ในเชิงจริยธรรม เราพึงมีความรับผิดชอบต่ออะไรบ้าง และเราจะรักษาอะไรไว้ให้เป็นมรดกแก่อนุชนรุ่นหลังบ้าง

แน่นอน สมัยนี้เป็นสมัยที่มีความสำคัญยิ่ง แม้จะทำการสื่อสารติดต่อกันได้ทั่วโลก แต่ก็มักจะเป็นการติดต่อเพื่อเผชิญหน้ากันมากกว่าที่จะมีการตกลงกันเพื่อสันติภาพอย่างแท้จริง

ขณะที่เราชื่นชมกับความก้าวหน้าทางวิทยาศาสตร์และเทคโนโลยี แต่เรากลับต้องเผชิญกับความทุกข์โศกและความหายนะที่ยิ่งใหญ่ไปกว่า รวมทั้งความอดอยากหิวโหยของมนุษย์ในโลก และการสูญพันธุ์ของสิ่งมีชีวิตอื่นๆ

การบุกเบิกสู่พิภพนอกโลกเป็นไปในเวลาเดียวกับที่มหาสมุทร ท้องทะเล และแหล่งน้ำจืดในโลกกำลังประสบกับภัยพิบัติอย่างใหญ่หลวง รวมทั้งความไม่รู้และความเข้าใจผิดต่อชีวิตในรูปแบบอื่น

ชีวิตต่างๆที่อาศัยอยู่บนโลก ไม่ว่าจะเป็นสัตว์ ต้นไม้ แมลง หรือจุลชีวะที่หาได้ยากนั้น อนุชนรุ่นหลังอาจไม่มีโอกาสได้รู้จักเลย

เรามีความสามารถและความรับผิดชอบ เราจะต้องเริ่มลงมือทำงานก่อนที่ทุกอย่างจะสายเกินไป

พระพุทธศาสนาและการอนุรักษ์ธรรมชาติ

ดร.ฉัตรสุมาลย์ กบิลสิงห์

วัดไผ่ล้อมเป็นวัดในพระพุทธศาสนาซึ่งอยู่ไม่ไกลจากกรุงเทพนัก และเป็นวัดที่ต้อนรับผู้มาเยือนจำนวนหลายพันที่มาจากแดนไกลในแต่ละปี ผู้มาเยือนที่ว่านี้ คือนกปากห่างนั่นเอง นกเหล่านี้จะมาพำนักที่วัดไผ่ล้อมในระหว่างฤดูใบไม้ผลิและฤดูหนาว มูลนกที่ถ่ายลงมาทำให้ต้นไม้และหลังคาวัดวาอารามในบริเวณนั้นดูขาวโพลนไปหมด

พระภิกษุสงฆ์ไม่มีท่าว่าจะรังเกียจ และบรรดาผู้ที่รักนกทั้งหลายก็พากันชื่นชมนกปากห่างที่กำลังจะสูญพันธุ์หากไม่มีสถานที่สำหรับฟักไข่ในบริเวณดังกล่าว

นักนิเวศฯวิทยาอธิบายถึงความจำเป็นในการที่จะต้องอนุรักษ์พันธุ์นกชนิดนี้ในเชิงวิทยาศาสตร์ว่า นกชนิดนี้ กินอาหารอย่างเดียว คือหอยทาก ซึ่งเป็นศัตรูสำคัญของข้าว หากไม่มีนกปากห่าง จำนวนหอยทากจะทวีจำนวนขึ้นมากมาย ทำให้ต้องหันไปใช้ยาฆ่าแมลงโดยไม่จำเป็น เป็นผลให้เกิดวัฏจักรมลพิษตามมา

จริยธรรมในพุทธศาสนามีส่วนสำคัญอย่างยิ่งต่อการอนุรักษ์พันธุ์นกปากห่างในประเทศไทย ใน 2-3 ทศวรรษที่ผ่านมา ประเทศไทยประสบปัญหาอย่างยิ่งในเรื่องการทำลายสิ่งแวดล้อมทางธรรมชาติ ตัวอย่าง เช่น ป่าไม้ซึ่งครอบคลุมเนื้อที่ร้อยละ 80 ของประเทศเมื่อ 50 ปีที่ผ่านมานี้ ปัจจุบันเนื้อที่ป่าไม้ลดลงเหลือเพียงร้อยละ 23 นก,สัตว์ และพืชพรรณไม้ต่างๆ กำลังตกอยู่ในอันตรายของการสูญพันธุ์ ในขณะที่บางชนิดก็ได้สูญพันธุ์ไปแล้ว

ความหายนะอันเป็นผลจากการทำลายธรรมชาติและแหล่งทรัพยากรธรรมชาติจะพบได้ในสังคมที่ต้องดิ้นรนเพื่อความอยู่รอด น้ำท่วมกรุงเทพทำให้เกิดความไม่สะดวกอย่างยิ่ง ในขณะที่ในภาคอิสาน ผลจากการทำลายธรรมชาติทำให้เกิดผลในทางตรงกันข้าม นั่นคือ ฝนไม่ตกต้องตามฤดูกาล ส่งผลกระทบถึงความอยู่รอดของประชาชนจำนวนไม่น้อย

ในขณะที่แหล่งทรัพยากรธรรมชาติหลายแห่งในประเทศไทยถูกทำลายลง แต่ก็เป็นที่น่าสังเกตุว่า ความสูญเสียอาจจะรุนแรงและแผ่ขยายไปในวงกว้างกว่าที่เป็นอยู่ เมื่อพิจารณาถึงความหื่นกระหายของโลกในการฉกฉวยผลประโยชน์โดยไม่คำนึงถึงผลเสียอันมหาศาลที่ตามมา

อาจเป็นไปได้ เช่นกรณีนกปากห่าง ว่าหลายอย่างที่ยังหลงเหลืออยู่ในธรรมชาติที่เป็น

อยู่นี้ มีความสัมพันธ์มากน้อยขึ้นอยู่กับอิทธิพลของพุทธศาสนา คำสอนซึ่งเน้นในความมีสติ ท่าทีและการกระทำที่ไม่เบียดเบียนผู้อื่น คำสอนเช่นนี้น่าจะเป็นผลอย่างยิ่งต่อการโอบอุ้มชีวิตบนพื้นโลก

ทั้งนี้มิได้หมายความว่า ปัจเจกบุคคลผู้ละโมภและกระทำการทำลายล้างธรรมชาตินั้นมิได้ถือตนว่าเป็นชาวพุทธ แต่เป็นเพราะจริยธรรมที่ว่าด้วยธรรมชาตินั้นต่างกันไปในแต่ละศาสนา และการตีความจริยธรรมนั้นก็แตกต่างกันไปในระดับบุคคล

ในระบบความเชื่อทั้งมวล ธรรมชาติของมนุษย์เป็นสิ่งที่ซับซ้อนยิ่ง ในพุทธศาสนาเองมีจำนวนศาสนิกทั่วโลกระหว่าง 300-600 ล้านคนนั้น ในบรรดาศาสนิกก็มีความแตกต่างกันอย่างยิ่ง นับตั้งแต่ผู้บรรลุธรรมขั้นสูง ผู้ที่มีศรัทธาในหลักศาสนา จนกระทั่งถึงกลุ่มผู้ที่ไม่รู้ว่าจะเรียกตนเองว่าอย่างไร กลุ่มนี้อาจจะเรียกได้ว่าเป็นชาวพุทธเพียงตามทะเบียนบ้าน

พุทธศาสนาสนับสนุนให้มีทรรศนะที่ต่างกันในระดับบุคคล อนุญาตให้มีการตั้งคำถามและการหาทายในระดับบุคคล ทั้งนี้เป็นเพราะการตรัสรู้ธรรมนั้นเป็นเรื่องของแต่ละบุคคล จากการศึกษาศาสนาเปรียบเทียบ พบว่า ลักษณะดังกล่าวเป็นลักษณะที่แปลกของพุทธศาสนา ขณะเดียวกัน พุทธศาสนาก็มีโครงสร้างสถาบันทางศาสนาที่เป็นหลักชัดเจน

ในคำสอนของพุทธศาสนานั้นเอง สิ่งสำคัญที่นักนิเวศน์วิทยาและนักอนุรักษ์สิ่งแวดล้อมเห็นว่า จำเป็นอย่างเร่งด่วน คือ การหยุดยั้งการทำลายล้างธรรมชาติและแหล่งทรัพยากรธรรมชาติ เพื่อว่าชีวิตบนโลกจะได้มีโอกาสอยู่ต่อไป

คำสอนต่างๆเน้นถึงความสำคัญของการอยู่ร่วมในธรรมชาติมากกว่าการเข้ายึดครอง ชาวพุทธที่แท้จริงย่อมพึงพอใจวิถีชีวิตที่เอื้ออำนวยชีวิตด้วยกันมากกว่าการบั่นทอนทำลายซึ่งกันและกัน

คำสอนสำคัญของพุทธศาสนาเน้นในเรื่องความเมตตากรุณา สนับสนุนให้มีความเคารพต่อชีวิตอื่นทั้งมนุษย์และสัตว์ร่วมโลก

ที่ใดก็ตาม ที่มีการปฏิบัติตามแนวพุทธศาสนา จากการศึกษาจะพบว่า ธรรมชาติย่อมได้รับผลประโยชน์โดยตรงในรูปแบบใดรูปแบบหนึ่ง ในประเทศศรีลังกาซึ่งมีประชากรส่วนใหญ่เป็นชาวพุทธ แม้จะมีมาตรฐานค่านิยมแบบตะวันตก แต่สัตว์ป่าก็ยังคงมีอยู่ จากการศึกษาพบว่า ที่เป็นเช่นนั้น เพราะประชากรส่วนใหญ่เป็นชาวพุทธในภาคปฏิบัติ

การอนุรักษ์ธรรมชาติในระบบนั้น โดยทั่วไปจะเป็นการทำงานของรัฐบาล แต่การ

กระทำดังกล่าว ย่อมไม่ส่งผลอย่างแท้จริง หากไม่มีการยอมรับในระดับประชาชน การอนุรักษ์ที่จะได้ผลอย่างแท้จริงจึงขึ้นอยู่กับการยอมรับและความเข้าใจในระดับปรัชญาชั้นพื้นฐาน

นักวิชาการชาวธิเบตหลายคนจะสามารถเล่าให้ฟังได้จากความทรงจำในชีวิตนี้ ถึงฝูงแกะ ฝูงจามรี ฝูงกวาง รวมทั้งฝูงนกจำนวนมากที่ท่องเที่ยวไปกับชาวธิเบต ท่ามกลางที่อยู่อาศัยของมนุษย์ ด้วยความรู้สึกปราศจากความกลัวภัย และที่เป็นเช่นนั้น เพราะชาวธิเบตเป็นชาวพุทธ

แต่น่าเสียดายที่สภาพการณ์ดังกล่าวเปลี่ยนไป ธิเบตในปัจจุบันกลายเป็นประเทศที่ระบบนิเวศน์วิทยาถูกทำลายลงในหลายรูปแบบ จากรายงานพิเศษของสหประชาชาติเรื่องสิทธิมนุษยชน ได้ระบุว่า พื้นที่ส่วนใหญ่ไม่มีป่าไม้ และ "สัตว์ป่าที่เคยมีอยู่อย่างอุดมสมบูรณ์ดูเหมือนจะสูญสิ้นไป"

ตลอดระยะเวลาในประวัติศาสตร์ที่ผ่านมา อาจกล่าวได้ว่าพุทธศาสนามีบทบาทต่อการอนุรักษ์ธรรมชาติเพียงในแง่ของการวางเฉย แต่เร็วๆนี้ ชาวพุทธที่มีอิทธิพลเริ่มกล่าวถึงเรื่องนี้มากขึ้น และพยายามทำให้เกิดการตระหนักในการที่จะทำให้พุทธศาสนามีบทบาทในเชิงปฏิภาคและมีพลังรุกมากขึ้นเพื่อเป็นประโยชน์ต่อการอนุรักษ์โดยตรง

องค์ดาไลลามะได้รับสั่งกับผู้สัมภาษณ์ว่า "ปัจจุบัน ยิ่งสำคัญกว่าที่แล้วมา ที่เราจะต้องให้ความสำคัญกับชีวิตโดยมีความรู้สึกรับผิดชอบร่วมกันเป็นสากล มิใช่เพียงระหว่างประเทศต่อประเทศ มนุษย์ต่อมนุษย์เท่านั้น แต่หมายรวมไปถึงมนุษย์และชีวิตรูปแบบอื่นๆด้วย"

สุลักษณ์ ศิวรักษ์ นักเขียนและนักวิจารณ์สังคม ผู้ซึ่งอาจนับได้ว่าเป็น "เสียงของชาวพุทธไทยในเรื่องของอาเซียและการเปลี่ยนแปลงของโลก" เชื่อว่า แม้โลกจะมีความซับซ้อนมากขึ้นเพียงใด คำสอนในพุทธศาสนาก็ยังคงมีอิทธิพล และน่าจะเป็นผู้นำที่สำคัญในเรื่องเอกภาพและความก้าวหน้าของสังคม"

ความตระหนักในความหายนะของการทำลายแหล่งทรัพยากรธรรมชาติ และด้วยความมั่นใจว่า พุทธศาสนาในบทบาทที่มีพลังรุกมากขึ้น จะนำไปสู่การพัฒนาการอนุรักษ์ ในภาพชุดสไลด์และเทปการบรรยายประกอบ เรื่องการตระหนักแบบพุทธ รวมทั้งท่าทีและการกระทำที่เกี่ยวข้องกับธรรมชาตินั้น อาจารย์สุลักษณ์ได้อธิบายว่า "ไม่ว่าจะโดยรู้ตัวหรือไม่ แต่นี่เป็นการปฏิวัติของชาวพุทธต่อการเสื่อมสลายของธรรมชาติ เป็นการปฏิวัติในกลุ่มเล็กๆ

เพราะยังไม่มีผลกระทบต่อมวลชน แต่แม้กระนั้น การปฏิวัติโดยสันติเช่นนี้ ย่อมบ่งชี้ถึงอะไรบางอย่าง และหากเอาจริงเอาจัง ก็จะสามารถนำไปสู่ขบวนการนักอนุรักษ์ในประเทศของเรา"

พณฯท่าน ยาสุฮิโร นากาโซเน่ นายกรัฐมนตรีของญี่ปุ่น ได้กล่าวในคำปราศัยครบรอบ 40 ปีขององค์การสหประชาชาติ เมื่อ พ.ศ. 2528 ในคำปราศัยนั้นได้เรียกร้องให้นานาชาติ ศาสนา และประชากรของโลก ได้ร่วมกันรักษาความงามและความหลากหลายตามธรรมชาติของโลกให้คงอยู่ต่อไป

และเราก็ได้พบอีกครั้งหนึ่งว่า ในคำปราศัยนั้น ได้นำพุทธศาสนาเข้ามาเพื่อสื่อข่าวสารในเรื่อง "จริยธรรมของโลกใหม่" เพื่อว่าศตวรรษที่ 20 จะได้เป็น "สมัยของการอยู่ร่วมและความเคารพซึ่งกันและกันในระหว่างประชาชนทั้งปวง และเป็นครั้งแรกที่มนุษย์ได้พบความสมดุลย์กับธรรมชาติ"

แม้คำสอนในพุทธศาสนาจะเป็นคำสอนที่มีมาแต่โบราณกาล ค่านิยมของพุทธศาสนาที่มีต่อชีวิตปัจจุบัน และความต้องการของสมัยนี้ก็เป็นที่ยอมรับกันมากขึ้น เหตุผลประการหนึ่งตามคำอธิบายของท่านอาจารย์ปิยทัสสี เป็นเพราะ "พระพุทธองค์ทรงเน้นภาคปฏิบัติ การนำความรู้ไปใช้ในชีวิต การพิจารณาชีวิตและไม่ได้หยุดลงเพียงนั้น"

เอช.จี.เวลส์ นักเขียนชาวอังกฤษ พบว่าเรื่องนี้ควรแก่การสนใจ และได้กล่าวว่า "คำสอนพื้นฐานของพระพุทธองค์ชัดเจนและมีความสอดคล้องใกล้ชิดกับแนวคิดสมัยใหม่ เป็นที่ยอมรับกันว่า เป็นคำสอนที่มีความเป็นเลิศทางปัญญาอย่างยิ่ง ที่โลกเคยรับรู้"

นอกจากนั้น พุทธศาสนายังได้อำนวยให้เกิดแนวทางใหม่ในทางการศึกษา นั่นคือ โครงการพุทธศาสนาเพื่อธรรมชาติ เป็นหน้าที่ของชาวพุทธผู้ปฏิบัติทั้งหลายที่จะทำลายล้างอวิชชาและแสวงหาปัญญาเข้ามาแทนที่ ในกรณีนี้ ครูอาจารย์เป็นผู้ที่ควรเคารพ และจะเป็นผู้นำในแนวความเชื่อได้เป็นอย่างดี

ในการเตรียมครูอาจารย์ให้พร้อมในด้านสื่อการสอน เพื่อครูจะได้สามารถนำนักเรียนในด้านการอนุรักษ์นั้น นักวิจัยของโครงการได้ศึกษาวิจัยคำสอนในพุทธศาสนาจากพระไตรปิฎกในภาษาต่างๆ

งานวิจัยเป็นงานขั้นแรก ต่อมาก็จะเป็นการรวบรวมข้อมูล นับเป็นครั้งแรกที่จะมีการรวบรวมคำสอนในพุทธศาสนาเกี่ยวกับความรับผิดชอบของมนุษย์ที่มีต่อสัตว์และพรรณพืช

ป่าไม้ แหล่งน้ำ อาจกล่าวได้ว่า เป็นการศึกษาเกี่ยวกับสภาพธรรมชาติทั้งมวลเพื่อรวบรวมลงในคู่มือการศึกษา

ข้อมูลจำนวนมากที่นักวิชาการได้ค้นพบนั้น ไม่น่าประหลาดใจเลย โดยเฉพาะเมื่อพิจารณาว่า พุทธศาสนาเองนั้น เน้นในเรื่องความเมตตากรุณา การอยู่ป่าและการบำเพ็ญสมาธิในสภาพธรรมชาติมีความจำเป็นยิ่งสำหรับคณะสงฆ์ รวมทั้งสัญลักษณ์ในพุทธศาสนาอันมีที่มาจากพืชและสัตว์ต่างๆ

โดยพระวินัยนั้น ห้ามมิให้พระสงฆ์ตัดต้นไม้ [8] ดังเรื่องที่เล่าถึงพระภิกษุรูปหนึ่งตัดกิ่งไม้ใหญ่ลง เทวดาที่สถิตอยู่ในต้นไม้ได้ทูลฟ้องต่อพระสัมมาสัมพุทธเจ้าว่า พระภิกษุตัดแขนลูกของตนดังนี้

คำสอนอีกตอนหนึ่ง กล่าวถึงผู้เดินทางในป่า เมื่อได้พักใต้ร่มเงาของไทรใหญ่แล้ว เวลาจะจากไป ก็กลับตัดกิ่งไม้นั้นลง การกระทำดังกล่าวเป็นสิ่งที่พุทธศาสนาประณามอย่างยิ่ง ด้วยต้นไม้นั้นได้ให้ร่มเงาดุจเพื่อน การทำร้ายเพื่อนจึงถือเป็นความชั่วอย่างยิ่ง

ใน<u>อังคุตตรนิกาย</u> มีเรื่องเล่าทำนองเดียวกันนี้

> "นานมาแล้ว พรหมธมิการาชาโกรันยะ มีต้นไทรใหญ่ต้นหนึ่ง เป็นต้นไม้ที่มีกิ่งก้านสาขาแผ่ขยายให้ร่มเงากว้างไกลถึง 12 โยชน์ ไม่มีผู้ใดคอยเฝ้ารักษา และไม่มีผู้ใดทำอันตราย"
>
> ต่อมามีชายคนหนึ่ง เก็บกินผลไม้จนเต็มอิ่ม หักรานกิ่งไม้แล้วจากไป เทวดาที่อาศัยอยู่ในต้นไม้นั้น รำพึงว่า น่าประหลาดจริงหนอ ที่มนุษย์จะชั่วช้าถึงกับหักรานกิ่งไม้ ทั้งๆที่ได้เก็บกินผลไม้จนอิ่มแล้วเช่นนั้น หากแม้นว่าต้นไม้นี้จะไม่ออกผลเล่า ....จากนั้น ต้นไม้นั้นก็ไม่ออกผลอีกต่อไป"

คำสอนดังกล่าวเตือนสติทั้งพระสงฆ์และชาวพุทธทั่วไป ถึงความสำคัญในการให้ความเคารพต่อต้นไม้ที่ออกดอกออกผล ให้ร่มเงาไม่เฉพาะแก่มนุษย์เท่านั้น แต่หมายถึงชีวิตในป่าทั้งปวงด้วย

ผลจากการขาดความเคารพต่อต้นไม้เป็นสิ่งที่เห็นได้ชัดเจนในทุกวันนี้ เมื่อป่าไม้บริเวณกว้างถูกทำลายลง ทำให้ผิวดินสึกกร่อน และในที่สุดทำให้เกษตรกรรมไร้ผล สัตว์และพรรณพืชไร้ที่อยู่อาศัยและสูญพันธุ์ไปในที่สุด

แม้ว่าพุทธศาสนาจะหยั่งรากในมนุษยชาติมากว่า 2500 ปี ในสมัยที่มนุษย์ยังมีความ

เป็นอยู่ใกล้ชิดกับธรรมชาติมากกว่าในปัจจุบัน แม้กระนั้นผลจากท่าทีและการกระทำอันไม่บังควรต่อโลกก็เกิดขึ้นแล้วในสมัยนั้น ดังปรากฏในเรื่องที่มีพราหมณ์ผู้หนึ่งทูลถามพระพุทธองค์ถึงสาเหตุของการลดน้อยถอยลงของมนุษย์ พระพุทธองค์รับสั่งตอบว่า

"เพราะมนุษย์เต็มไปด้วยความละโมภอันผิดกฎหมาย ถูกครอบงำด้วยความอยาก และถูกชักนำด้วยทุคติ เมื่อเป็นเช่นนั้น ฝนก็ไม่ตกต้องตามฤดูกาล การหากินเป็นไปด้วยความยากลำบาก ผลผลิตน้อย และไม่ได้ผล เช่นนี้ หลายคนก็พบกับความวิบัติ"

ตามอุดมคติแล้ว ชาวพุทธที่เคร่งครัดรักษาศีลไม่เบียดเบียนชีวิตผู้อื่น จะใช้ชีวิตอยู่ด้วยการกินผลไม้และพืชผัก และในการปฏิบัติดังกล่าว ก็จะต้องมีสติเป็นสำคัญ

ในการกินผลไม้และพืชผักนั้น พระสงฆ์และชาวพุทธผู้เคร่งครัดพึงระวังในการที่จะไม่ทำลายการเจริญเติบโตของอาหารนั้น ดังนั้นพระสงฆ์จึงฉันได้เฉพาะผลไม้ที่เอาเมล็ดออกแล้ว เป็นต้น

พระวินัยในเรื่องอาหารการกินมีความซับซ้อนมาก ในงานวิจัยได้ศึกษาเรื่องนี้โดยละเอียด ประเด็นที่ควรสนใจในหนังสือแนะนำเช่นเล่มนี้ ขอกล่าวโดยย่อเพียงว่า ในการกระทำทั้งมวลของมนุษย์นั้น จะต้องมีความเคารพต่อชีวิตอื่น ด้วยความตระหนักในการอนุรักษ์และงดเว้นการฉกฉวยตักตวงเพื่อการทำลาย

ในพุทธศาสนานั้น สัตว์ทั้งปวงล้วนอยู่ในทรรศนะวิสัยของมนุษย์ เพราะในอนาคตสัตว์เหล่านั้นก็มีโอกาสบรรลุความรู้แจ้งเช่นกัน มนุษย์แม้ว่าจะถือกันว่าเป็นสัตว์ประเสริฐ แต่พุทธศาสนาก็ถือว่า มนุษย์ก็เป็นส่วนหนึ่งของธรรมชาติทั้งปวงเช่นกัน การฝ่าฝืนกฎเกณฑ์ของธรรมชาติ หรือความพยายามที่จะเป็นเจ้าธรรมชาติจึงเป็นการทำลายตนเอง

พระภิกษุกรรมะ เกเล็ก ยูทอก หัวหน้านักวิชาการฝ่ายธิเบตในโครงการพุทธศาสนาเพื่อธรรมชาติ ได้เสนอข้อคิดเกี่ยวกับความเมตตาต่อสรรพสัตว์ทางฝ่ายมหายานว่า

"คำสอนของสมเด็จพระสัมมาสัมพุทธเจ้า เน้นในเรื่องความเมตตา ผู้ที่ยึดพระพุทธศาสนาเป็นสรณะ จึงควรมีจิตเมตตาละเว้นการทำอันตรายต่อชีวิตอื่นด้วย"

ในการอธิบายความสำคัญในการงดเว้นการเบียดเบียนชีวิตอื่น ทสองขะปะ สอนว่า

"การงดเว้นการทำอันตรายชีวิตอื่น เป็นการเว้นจากความคิดและการกระ

ทำทั้งปวง....เช่นการเฆี่ยนตีมนุษย์และสัตว์ ผูกล่ามด้วยเชือก ทำกับดักหรือกรงขัง เจาะร้อยรูจมูก บรรทุกของหนักเกินควร และการกระทำทำนองนี้"

ในทำนองเดียวกัน ชอกเซ็น ปาตุล จิกเม วังโม ในหนังสือของท่านเรื่อง <u>วจนะของพระสมานตภัทร</u> นั้น กล่าวว่า

"ดังที่ได้กล่าวแล้ว ว่าการยึดพระธรรมเป็นสรณะนั้น จะต้องงดเว้นการทำอันตรายชีวิตทั้งปวง การกระทำที่เป็นอันตรายต่อชีวิตอื่นนั้น จะต้องยกเลิก และไม่ให้เกิดขึ้นแม้ในความฝัน....ต้องทำความเพียรอย่างยิ่งที่จะปกป้องตนเองจากการกระทำดังกล่าว"

การไม่ทำอันตรายต่อชีวิตนั้น เป็นขั้นหนึ่งเพื่อก้าวไปสู่ท่าทีแบบพุทธที่พึงมีต่อชีวิตทั้งมวล นั่นคือ ความมีเมตตากรุณา และในท่าทีของความมีเมตตากรุณานั้น พระพุทธองค์ทรงสอนว่า

"ในการถวายทานอันมหาศาลที่มีในสหัสโลกธาตุต่อผู้ประเสริฐทั้งหลายนั้น แม้ทานนั้นก็ไม่ยิ่งใหญ่เท่ากับการมีจิตเมตตากรุณาแม้เพียงขณะหนึ่ง"

คำสอนที่เป็นที่รู้จักและยกย่องกันทั่วไปอีกตอนหนึ่ง ซึ่งแสดงให้เห็นถึงคำสอนในเรื่องความเมตตาในพุทธศาสนา ได้แก่

"ดุจเดียวกับมารดาที่พิทักษ์ชีวิตของบุตรน้อย ขอให้ท่านมีความคิดที่จะคุ้มครองชีวิตทั้งปวง"

สองพันกว่าปีมาแล้วที่พระพุทธองค์ทรงสอนสาวกทั้งหลายว่า วัตถุธาตุนี้ คือทั้งโลกและจักรวาล รวมทั้งรูปธรรมทั้งปวงทั้งชีวิตและบรรยากาศ คำสอนเก่าแก่นี้เทียบได้กับความรู้ทางชีวภาพซึ่งจัดเป็นความรู้แขนงใหม่ที่ก้าวหน้ายิ่ง แม้กระนั้นก็ยังมีความสำคัญเป็นรองสำหรับชาวพุทธในเรื่องความ จำเป็นที่จะต้องเผยแผ่ท่าทีอันเปี่ยมด้วยความเมตตากรุณานี้

หลายศตวรรษก่อนที่จะมีปัญหาเรื่องน้ำเสียจนกลายเป็นปัญหาคุกคามสุขภาพและชีวิตมนุษย์อย่างกว้างขวางดังที่เป็นอยู่ในทุกวันนี้ พระพุทธองค์ได้ทรงวางเป็นพระวินัยของสงฆ์แล้วในการห้ามมิให้ทำน้ำเสีย แม้จนกระทั่งในรายละเอียดของการสร้างห้องน้ำให้ถูกวิธี ล้วนแล้วแต่เป็นการสะท้อนให้เห็นถึงความสำคัญและการตระหนักในการอนุรักษ์ธรรมชาติทั้งสิ้น

ในสมัยที่พุทธศาสนารุ่งเรืองนั้น เป็นสมัยที่อยู่ในสภาพแวดล้อมทางธรรมชาติอันอุดมสมบูรณ์ จึงปรากฏในคำสอนถึงการใช้ธรรมชาติมาเปรียบเทียบยกเป็นตัวอย่างในการอธิบายคำสอนที่สำคัญ

"เปรียบได้กับสระน้ำอันขุ่นมีโคลนตม จิตของมนุษย์ที่สกปรกก็เป็นดุจเดียวกัน เช่นเดียวกับสระน้ำที่สะอาดและใสบริสุทธิ์ จนสามารถมองเห็นหอยและปู ก้อนกรวด ก้อนหินจนกระทั่งฝูงปลาได้ฉันใด จิตของมนุษย์อันบริสุทธิ์แล้วก็เป็นเช่นนั้น"

เมื่ออธิบายถึงจิตระดับต่างๆจนกระทั่งบรรลุพระธรรมะก็ใช้สัญลักษณ์ดอกบัวอันเป็นดอกไม้ที่นิยมกันทั้งในหมู่ชาวฮินดูและชาวพุทธ

"ดุจเดียวกัน ในสระที่มีบัวสีน้ำเงิน สีแดงและสีขาว ดอกบัวสีน้ำเงิน สีแดงและสีขาวบางดอก เกิดในน้ำ เจริญในน้ำ แต่ไม่โผล่พ้นผิวน้ำ ยังจมอยู่กับน้ำ ในขณะที่ดอกบัวสีน้ำเงิน สีแดง และสีขาวบางดอก เกิดในน้ำ เจริญในน้ำ โผล่ขึ้นพ้นผิวน้ำ ไร้มลทิน"

สัตว์ที่รู้จักดีในป่าหลายชนิด ก็ปรากฏในคำสอนของสมเด็จพระสัมมาสัมพุทธเจ้าเช่นกัน เช่น เสือ ช้าง และราชสีห์ เป็นต้น คำสอนที่เกี่ยวกับสัตว์เหล่านี้ เป็นคำสอนที่ย้ำในความเมตตากรุณา และในบางแห่งพระองค์ยังได้ทรงเปรียบเทียบพระอิริยาบทของพระองค์เองกับราชสีห์..."พระองค์ทรงแสดงสีหนาท ประกาศว่าจะไม่ล่วงแม้ชีวิตสัตว์เล็กน้อย"...คำว่าราชสีห์บางครั้งใช้กับพระพุทธองค์ด้วยซ้ำไป

ในวรรณคดีพุทธศาสนามีเรื่องราวบางตอนที่แสดงถึงการพึ่งพาอาศัยและการอยู่ร่วมกันระหว่างมนุษย์กับสัตว์ ในพุทธศาสนาได้ตระหนักว่า ความอยู่รอดของสัตว์บางเผ่าพันธุ์กำลังอยู่ในอันตราย และการสูญเสียชีวิตสัตว์หมายถึงการสิ้นสุดของโลก

นักวิชาการของสมาคมบาลีปกรณ์แห่งกรุงลอนดอน ได้แปลข้อความตอนนี้ไว้อย่างงดงาม ปรากฏใน ขุทธกบาท ว่า

"จงกลับมาเถิด เสือทั้งหลาย กลับมาสู่ป่าเถิด ถ้าไม่มีป่า ก็จะไม่มีการตัดไม้ทำลายป่า แต่หากเจ้าขาดป่า เจ้าก็จะไร้บ้านตลอดไป"

พุทธศาสนาชื่นชมกับความอุดมสมบูรณ์และความหลากหลายของธรรมชาติในโลก ดอกบัวเป็นพรรณไม้ชนิดหนึ่งที่มีความสำคัญยิ่งในเชิงสัญลักษณ์

ในพระไตรปิฎกได้บันทึกว่า เจ้าชายสิทธัตถะประสูติในป่า ภายใต้ร่มไม้ และตามพุทธประวัติเล่าว่า ทันทีที่ประสูติได้ดำเนินไป 7 ก้าว ทุกๆก้าวที่ดอกบัวขึ้นมารอง

รับ และเมื่อทรงบำเพ็ญสมาธิในวัยเด็ก ก็ประทับนั่งใต้ต้นหว้า ซึ่งมีพันธุ์ต่างๆถึง 650 ชนิด จากการศึกษาพันธุ์ไม้ชนิดต่างๆเหล่านี้ เราจะพบว่า บทบาทความศรัทธามีส่วนในการอนุรักษ์อยู่มาก เพราะคุณค่าอันเป็นสัญลักษณ์ซึ่งปรากฏในชีวิตของพระพุทธเจ้า ต้นไม้เหล่านี้จึงได้รับการเคารพ และชาวพุทธโดยทั่วไปจะไม่จงใจทำลายต้นไม้เหล่านี้

ในงานวิจัยของเรา มีข้อที่น่าสนใจที่จะขอกล่าวถึง นั่นคือ ดูเหมือนจะมีวิธีกล่าวถึงธรรมชาติอยู่ 2 แบบ เป็นการอธิบายและกล่าวถึงธรรมชาติโดยตรงแบบหนึ่ง ในขณะที่อีกหลายๆตอนเป็นการเปรียบเทียบ

แต่ทั้งสองแบบก็มาจากชีวิตและสิ่งแวดล้อมตามธรรมชาติของสมัยนั้น และในทางตอนเหนือของประเทศอินเดีย ได้แสดงให้เห็นถึงความเข้าใจในเรื่อง การพึ่งพาอาศัยซึ่งกันและกันของชีวิตทั้งหลาย จะเห็นได้ชัดเจนว่า ชาวพุทธในสมัยแรก เป็นผู้รักธรรมชาติอย่างแท้จริง

ใน<u>สุตตนิบาต</u> ซึ่งเป็นคำสอนที่เก่าแก่ส่วนหนึ่ง พระพุทธองค์ได้รับสั่งว่า

> "ให้รู้จักต้นหญ้าและต้นไม้ แม้จะไม่มีปัจจัยแห่งพันธุ์ปรากฏ แต่มันก็มีพันธุ์ต่างๆมากมาย
>
> ให้รู้จักตัวหนอนและตัวแมลง และมดชนิดต่างๆ...
>
> จงรู้จักสัตว์ 4 เท้า ทั้งเล็กและใหญ่...
>
> จงรู้จักงูชนิดต่างๆ....
>
> จงรู้จักปลาต่างพันธุ์ในน้ำ...
>
> จงรู้จักนกที่มีปีกและบินในอากาศ...
>
> สัตว์ต่างๆเหล่านี้ มีชนิดพันธุ์มากมาย ในมนุษย์ก็เช่นกัน...

ในนิทานชาดกก็เต็มไปด้วยเรื่องเล่าที่มีความไพเราะ บรรยายถึงความงามของธรรมชาติ เนื้อเรื่องที่กล่าวถึงในตอนที่ 4 และ 5 ได้กล่าวถึงอย่างชื่นชมถึงป่าและน้ำรวมทั้งสัตว์ป่าด้วย

สวนแห่งความรื่นรมย์ที่กล่าวถึงบนพื้นโลกนั้น จะมีต้นหญ้าขึ้นอยู่เขียวขจี ในป่าจะมีต้นไม้ที่ออกผลให้มนุษย์ได้ลิ้มรส และน้ำในลำธารก็สะอาดและมีรสหวาน มีสีฟ้าดุจแก้วมณี มีปลาว่ายเป็นฝูงในบริเวณใกล้กันนั้น...

> "เป็นดินแดนที่งดงาม เต็มไปด้วยต้นไม้ และพันธุ์ไม้เลื้อยออกดอกสะพรั่ง มีเสียงร้องของหงส์ เป็ด และห่าน และเป็นที่อยู่ของพระ

ภิกษุและนักพรตนักบวช"

อีกตอนหนึ่งได้กล่าวถึงดินแดน "อันอุดม มีพันธุ์ไม้ต่างๆ มีดอกไม้พันธุ์ต่างๆขึ้นกระจายอยู่ทั่วไป" และสัตว์ป่าชนิดต่างๆ มีเลียงผา ช้าง ควาย กวาง จามรี สิงโต แรด เสือ เสือดาว หมี สุนัขป่า นาก กระต่ายป่า และอื่นๆ

หากจะมีภาพที่ไม่งดงามนัก ก็เป็นเพราะความโง่เขลา ความโลภ และขาดความเคารพต่อโลก จำนวนประชากรของโลกที่เพิ่มขึ้น ทำให้สวนแห่งความรื่นรมย์ที่กล่าวมาข้างต้นนั้น กลายเป็นบริเวณที่แห้งแล้ง ขาดความสมบูรณ์ตามธรรมชาติลง

โลกได้ถูกทำลายไปเป็นจำนวนมาก และการทำลายล้างยังคงดำเนินต่อไป โดยไม่สัมพันธ์กับคำสอนทางศาสนาและความเชื่อทางศาสนาที่แสวงหาความรู้และความแจ้ง และศาสนิกที่รู้สึกรับผิดชอบต่อสภาพของโลกและอนาคตของอนุชนรุ่นต่อๆไป

ในงานวิจัยโครงการพุทธศาสนาเพื่อธรรมชาติ เราได้ค้นพบและรวบรวมคำสอนซึ่งแสดงว่า เราได้สูญเสียโลกแห่งธรรมชาติไปมากเพียงใดในเวลาอันสั้น นี่เป็นบทเรียนที่สำคัญที่เราต้องเรียนรู้ และยิ่งทำให้เพิ่มพูนความรู้สึกที่ว่า งานวิจัยของเราเป็นสิ่งจำเป็นและเร่งด่วน และจะต้องมีวัสดุสื่อการสอนที่ดีสำหรับบรรดาครูอาจารย์ที่จะใช้ให้เป็นประโยชน์

ในการทำงานในส่วนของเราเพื่อนำคำสอนในพุทธศาสนามาเป็นแสงสว่างนำทางในปัจจุบัน ในวงการพุทธศาสนาที่กว้างขึ้น น่าจะเป็นปัจจัยสำคัญในการอนุรักษ์สิ่งแวดล้อมทางธรรมชาติที่ถูกต้อง

โดยการนำผลงานวิจัยของเรามาเผยแผ่ให้กับผู้อื่น เราคาดหวังว่าจะได้รับการยอมรับในระดับโลก ในการสร้างจริยธรรมนิเวศน์วิทยา เป็นการนำความรู้เข้ามาแทนที่ความโง่เขลา ความเอื้อเฟื้อเผื่อแผ่เข้ามาแทนที่ความละโมภ ความเมตตากรุณาต่อชีวิตทั้งมวลเข้ามาแทนที่การขาดความเคารพที่พึงมีต่อโลก

ธันวาคม พ.ศ.2529

ดร.ฉัตรสุมาลย์ กบิลสิงห์ เป็นหัวหน้านักวิชาการ ในโครงการพระพุทธศาสนาเพื่อธรรมชาติ เป็นรองศาสตราจารย์ในคณะศิลปศาสตร์ มหาวิทยาลัยธรรมศาสตร์ กรุงเทพ เป็นผู้เขียนบทความเกี่ยวกับพุทธศาสนาและสตรีหลายชิ้น เป็นผู้แปล <u>สัทธรรมปุณฑริกสูตร</u>, <u>คัมภีร์เต๋า</u> ฯลฯ หนังสือทางวิชาการที่สำคัญได้แก่ <u>การศึกษาเปรียบเทียบภิกษุณีปาฏิโมกข์</u>

สภาวะสิ่งแวดล้อมในปัจจุบัน
และความต้องการในอนาคต

ดร. เน ทูน

ในช่วง ๓๐ ปีที่ผ่านมา โลกเราได้ประสบกับความเจริญเติบโตอย่างหาที่เปรียบไม่ได้ และด้วยเหตุดังกล่าว แหล่งทรัพยากรธรรมชาติหมดสิ้นไปโดยเร็ว ทำให้ระบบการครองชีพและสภาวะแวดล้อมต้องได้รับผลกระทบกระเทือนตามไปด้วย จึงทำให้เกิดความกังวลว่าความเปลี่ยนแปลงเหล่านี้ จะมีผลกระทบอย่างรุนแรงชนิดที่แก้ไขไม่ได้เกิดขึ้นแก่โลก

อัตราความเร็วของการเปลี่ยนแปลงจะเห็นได้จากสถิติที่น่าตกใจ เมื่อเราพบว่าทุก ๆ ๒๐ ปี เราจะสูญเสียเนื้อที่ทำการเพาะปลูก ๒๐ ล้านเฮกแตร์ เนื้อที่ป่าถูกทำลาย ๑๒ ล้านเฮกแตร์ และเนื้อดินเป็นจำนวนถึง ๒๕ พันล้านตันถูกทำลายลง และเนื้อดินอีก ๓๐๐๐ พันล้านเฮกแตร์สูญเสียไปกับการทำเหมือง

ในขณะเดียวกัน อัตราการใช้น้ำก็เพิ่มขึ้นจาก ๓,๐๐๐ ลูกบาศก์กิโลเมตร ใน พ.ศ. ๒๕๒๓ เป็น ๓,๗๕๐ ใน พ.ศ.๒๕๒๘ การใช้เชื้อเพลิงในการอุตสาหกรรมต้องการน้ำมันถึง ๗,๕๐๐ พันล้านเมตริกตัน เป็นจำนวนเกือบ ๒๐ เท่าตัวของอัตราที่เคยใช้เมื่อ ๒๐ ปีก่อน จำนวนยวดยานพาหนะก็เพิ่มจาก ๕๐ ล้าน ใน พ.ศ. ๒๔๙๐ เป็น ๔๑๐ ล้าน ในต้นปี พ.ศ.๒๕๒๓ ที่สำคัญที่สุด ก็คือจำนวนประชากรในปัจจุบันเพิ่มขึ้น ๑ พันล้านคน ทุก ๑๕ ปี นั่นหมายความว่าในปลายศตวรรษนี้ เราจะมีประชากรของโลกสูงถึง ๖ พันล้านคน เป็นจำนวน ๒ เท่าของจำนวนประชากรเมื่อ พ.ศ. ๒๕๒๓

จำนวนตัวเลขเหล่านี้อาจทำให้เกิดความมึนชาในสมอง แต่ก็เป็นที่แน่ชัดว่าโลกนี้กลายเป็นเบี้ยล่าง ถูกตักตวง และเอารัดเอาเปรียบอย่างสุดประมาณ การตักตวงทรัพยากรจากพื้นผิวโลกในรูปแบบต่าง ๆ ทำให้โลกเองหมดพลังในการพลิกฟื้นและเยียวยาตนเอง

ในบทความนี้ ข้าพเจ้าจะแสดงให้เห็นถึงภาพกว้าง ๆ ในสภาวะแวดล้อมของอากาศ น้ำ ดิน และป่าไม้ จะได้กล่าวถึงวิธีการทางเทคนิค ทางเศรษฐกิจ และมาตรการ

จากองค์การต่าง ๆ ในความพยายามที่จะต่อสู้กับแนวโน้มนี้ และในท้ายสุดจะได้เสนอแนะมาตรการเพื่อการนำไปสู่การพัฒนา โดยมิได้จำกัดเฉพาะมาตรฐานการครองชีพเท่านั้นแต่ยังหมายรวมไปถึงคุณภาพชีวิต โดยการใช้ทรัพยากรอย่างสมเหตุสมผล และให้มีผลกระจายต่อสภาพแวดล้อมน้อยที่สุด –โดยย่อเป็นการพัฒนาเพื่อให้คงสภาพอยู่ได้

โดยสรุป ข้าพเจ้าอยากสนับสนุนให้มีการใช้จริยธรรมในเรื่องความเมตตากรุณา ความอดทน และความเคารพต่อชีวิตในรูปแบบต่าง ๆ และความรับผิดชอบที่พึงมีต่อพื้นโลก

สภาวะสิ่งแวดล้อม

ปัจจุบัน เราสามารถแสวงหาข้อมูลและสถิติเกี่ยวกับสิ่งแวดล้อมได้มากขึ้น ใน พ.ศ. ๒๕๒๕ โครงการสิ่งแวดล้อมของสหประชาชาติ (UNEP) ได้ศึกษาโดยละเอียดถึงสภาวะสิ่งแวดล้อม และโครงการนี้ ได้พิมพ์เผยแพร่รายงานประจำปีเกี่ยวกับสภาวะสิ่งแวดล้อม โดยมุ่งเน้นที่หัวข้อประเด็นต่าง ๆ ในทำนองเดียวกัน บราวน์ (พ.ศ. ๒๕๒๙) ก็ได้เสนอรายงานประจำปีสภาวะของโลก และเมื่อเร็ว ๆ นี้ สถาบันทรัพยากรของโลก (พ.ศ. ๒๕๒๙) ก็ได้ประเมินแหล่งทรัพยากรพื้นฐาน ที่สนับสนุนเศรษฐกิจของโลกทั้งมวล นอกจากนั้น ก็ยังมีรายงานสภาวะสิ่งแวดล้อมในระดับชาติ จากประเทศต่าง ๆ อีกด้วย

บรรยากาศ

โลกปัจจุบันกำลังเผชิญหน้ากับปัญหาคุณภาพของอากาศ เช่นฝนกรด และการทำลายชั้นบรรยากาศของโอโซน

ฝนเหลือง เป็นปรากฏการณ์ที่เกิดขึ้นเมื่อ ซัลเฟอร์กับไนโตรเจนออกไซด์ถูกขับออกมาจากแรงกดของพลังขับเคลื่อนของเชื้อเพลิงที่เกิดจากซากพืชและสัตว์และแหล่งทรัพยากรธรรมชาติ เช่น การระเบิดของภูเขาไฟ ที่ขึ้นไปรวมตัวอยู่ในเมฆหมอกแล้วทำให้ฝนและหิมะกลายเป็นกรด ประมาณ ๑๘๐ พันล้านตันของอ็อกไซด์ประเภทนี้ถูกขับออกมาในแต่ละปี และแผ่ขยายออกไปเป็นวงกว้างกว่า ๑,๐๐๐ กิโลเมตร

การที่เกิดปลาตายในทะเลสาปของสแกนดิเนเวีย และอเมริกาเหนือ มีสาเหตุโดยตรงจากการทิ้งโลหะที่มีพิษลงบนพื้นดิน แม้จะยังไม่มีการเห็นพ้องกันว่าฝนเหลืองเป็นสาเหตุของการสูญเสียเหล่านี้ และรวมไปถึงการทำลายป่าไม้ในยุโรป แต่ก็มีการยอมรับกันมากขึ้นว่านี่เป็นเหตุสำคัญประการหนึ่ง โดยตรงหรือโดยอ้อมก็ตามในการทำให้ระบบการทำงานอย่างอื่นย่อหย่อนตามลงไปด้วย การกระจายตัวของกรดเหล่านี้ ทำให้ตึกรามบ้านช่อง อนุสาวรีย์ และอนุสรณ์สถานเสื่อมเร็วกว่าที่ควร เหล็กผุกร่อนเร็วขึ้น ทำให้ต้องทาสีบ่อยขึ้น และทำให้เศรษฐกิจและวัฒนธรรมมีราคาสูงขึ้นเป็นเงาตามตัว

เมื่อหันไปพิจารณาการสร้าง "greenhouse gases" ในขณะนี้มีเหตุผลชัดเจนที่ทำให้เชื่อได้ว่า มีการรวมตัวของกาซมากขึ้น เช่น คาร์บอนไดออกไซด์ คาร์บอนมอนนอกไซด์ มีเธน ไนตรัสออกไซด์ และคลอโรฟลูโรคาร์บอนด์ ซึ่งควบคุมชั้นของโอโซนของโลกซึ่งจะทำให้อุณหภูมิความร้อนสูงขึ้น อันเป็นผลมาจากกาซเรือนกระจก (greenhouse gases) ถ้าจะกล่าวโดยนัยของปริมาณ การรวมตัวของคาร์บอนไดออกไซด์สูงกว่ากาซอื่นทั้งหมด ระหว่าง พ.ศ. ๒๔๔๓ – ๒๕๒๓ เพิ่มขึ้นด้วยอัตราโดยเฉลี่ยร้อยละ ๔ ต่อปี

ถ้าจะกล่าวโดยหลักแล้ว กาซเรือนกระจก ทำให้เกิดผลกระทบทางด้านชั้นของบรรยากาศ นั่นคือทำให้รังสีจากแสงอาทิตย์เข้ามากระทบโลกได้มากขึ้น รังสีบางส่วนกลืนหายไปในบรรยากาศชั้นนอก และบางส่วนถูกดึงดูดไว้โดยกาซเรือนกระจก ทำให้อุณหภูมิในโลกสูงขึ้น

การที่อุณหภูมิบนพื้นผิวโลกสูงขึ้นนี้ เรารู้มาล่วงหน้าตั้งแต่ พ.ศ. ๒๔๔๓ แล้ว ในช่วงทศวรรษที่ผ่านมา มีการศึกษาค้นคว้าในเรื่องนี้เพิ่มมากขึ้น และในการประชุมในเรื่องกาซเรือนกระจก และการเปลี่ยนแปลงของอุณหภูมิและผลข้างเคียงของ UNEP/WMO/ICSU จัดขึ้นเมื่อ พ.ศ. ๒๕๒๘ ในประเทศออสเตรียนั้น ได้มีมติสากลว่า ถ้ามวลคาร์บอนไดออกไซด์สูงขึ้นอีกเท่าตัว อุณหภูมิของโลกจะเพิ่มขึ้นในอัตรา ๑.๕ ถึง ๔.๕ องศาเซนติเกรด ลมและคลื่นลมในทะเลจะเปลี่ยนไป ทำให้ระดับน้ำทะเลสูงขึ้นอีก ระหว่าง ๒๐ – ๑๔๐ เซนติเมตร และเมืองชายทะเลหลายเมืองจะจมน้ำ นอกจากนี้ก็จะมีผลกระทบในด้านนิเวศน์วิทยาของโลก มีผลกระทบต่อด้านเกษตรกรรมและแหล่งน้ำ ทำให้เกิดผลกระทบอย่างรุนแรงต่อสังคมเศรษฐกิจ

เมื่อชั้นของโอโซนถูกรบกวนในบรรยากาศชั้นสูง โอโซนจะดูดซึมรังสีคลื่นสั้นอุลตราไวโอเล็ต แล้วจะปล่อยให้รังสีคลื่นยาวซึ่งมีอันตรายมากกว่าลงมาสู่พื้นผิวโลก แต่เมื่อชั้นของโอโซนถูกทำลายลงในที่สุด รังสีอุลตราไวโอเล็ตก็จะผ่านชั้นของบรรยากาศเข้ามาเช่นกัน

ตัวการที่ทำลายชั้นของโอโซนที่สำคัญคือ ไนโตรเจนออกไซด์ ๒ ชนิด ผลกระทบโดยตรงที่เห็นชัดจะเกิดกับผิวของมนุษย์ ที่เห็นง่ายที่สุดคือผิวที่ถูกแดดจนไหม้เกรียม และยังทำให้เกิดมะเร็งผิวหนัง ๒ ชนิด ชนิดหนึ่งเป็นอันตรายอย่างยิ่ง

เมื่อรังสีอุลตราไวโอเล็ตลงมากระทบผิวโลกมากขึ้นก็จะมีผลทางด้านเกษตรกรรม หน่วยงานของสหรัฐอเมริกาด้านการประเมินความสูญเสียในพืชไร่ รายงานว่า ในพื้นที่จำกัดที่ชั้นของโอโซนต่ำ ผลผลิตถั่วลิสงจะน้อยกว่าธรรมดาถึง ๕๐% การเปลี่ยนแปลงในชั้นของโอโซนจะทำให้เกิดผลกระทบต่ออัตราความร้อน การเคลื่อนตัวของอากาศ การส่องผ่านของรังสีอินฟราเรด และการระเหยของน้ำ ฯลฯ

<u>น้ำและการใช้น้ำ</u>

มวลน้ำทั้งหมดซึ่งมีอยู่ ๑,๔๐๐ ล้านลูกบาศก์กิโลเมตรนั้น มีการเปลี่ยนแปลงน้อยมาก อย่างไรก็ตามประมาณร้อยละ ๙๗ ของน้ำทั้งหมดเป็นน้ำทะเล น้ำสะอาดที่จะใช้ได้ทันทีนั้นมีเพียงร้อยละ ๐.๐๑ ส่วนที่เหลือถูกจำกัดอยู่ในขั้วโลกเหนือ ซึ่งลึกลงไปถึง ๗๕๐ เมตร หรือมิฉะนั้นก็มีสภาพเป็นไอน้ำอยู่ในชั้นของบรรยากาศ และน้ำจำนวนน้อยนิดที่มนุษย์เราจะใช้ได้นี้ ก็ถูกใช้อย่างทิ้ง ๆ ขว้าง ๆ

เราไม่มีตัวเลขที่แน่ชัดเกี่ยวกับการใช้น้ำ แต่จากการประเมินอย่างคร่าว ๆ พบว่าใน พ.ศ.๒๕๒๘ เราใช้น้ำประมาณ ๓,๐๐๐ ลูกบาศก์กิโลเมตร ใช้ไปในด้านเกษตรกรรมร้อยละ ๗๓ อุตสาหกรรมร้อยละ ๒๑ และใช้ภายในครัวเรือนร้อยละ ๖

พื้นที่ที่ใช้น้ำเพื่อเกษตรกรรมทั่วโลกขยายไปจาก ๒๘ ล้าน ถึง ๕๐ ล้านเฮกแตร์ระหว่าง พ.ศ. ๒๕๐๓ – ๒๕๒๘ แม้ว่าจะใช้น้ำมากขนาดนี้ แต่ก็ได้ผลเพียงร้อยละ ๓๐–๕๐ เท่านั้น การใช้น้ำจากพื้นโลกในบริเวณที่แห้งแล้ง และระบบการใช้น้ำที่ไม่ถูกต้องได้ทำให้เกิดปัญหาน้ำเค็ม น้ำเป็นกรด และน้ำขัง

การใช้น้ำในด้านอุตสาหกรรมในประเทศที่พัฒนาแล้วมีอัตราลดลงในทศวรรษที่ผ่านมา ที่เป็นเช่นนี้เพราะความสัมฤทธิผลในการใช้น้ำหมุนเวียน ในสหรัฐอเมริกา ญี่ปุ่น และเยอรมนีตะวันตก จะใช้น้ำในโรงงาน ๒ ครั้งก่อนที่จะปล่อยทิ้ง แต่ในประเทศที่กำลังพัฒนาอัตราการใช้น้ำกลับสูงขึ้นตามอัตราการเจริญเติบโตของอุตสาหกรรม จึงมีความจำเป็นเร่งด่วนที่จะต้องใช้มาตรการการถนอมการใช้น้ำ

การใช้น้ำในครัวเรือน น้ำดื่ม น้ำเพื่อชำระล้าง ฯลฯ แม้จะมีอัตราส่วนจำนวนน้อยเมื่อเทียบกับการใช้น้ำทั้งหมดแล้ว แต่ก็มีผลกระทบที่สำคัญต่อสุขภาพของมนุษย์ ประชากรทุก ๓ ใน ๕ คน ในประเทศกำลังพัฒนาไม่มีน้ำดื่มที่สะอาดเพียงพอ และประชาชนประมาณ ๒ พันล้านคนได้รับเชื้อโรคจากน้ำดื่มที่ไม่สะอาดเพียงพอ สำหรับในด้านการสุขาภิบาลนั้น ประชากรทุก ๓ ใน ๕ คนของประเทศที่กำลังพัฒนายังไม่มีระบบสุขาภิบาล

ปัญหาการทำน้ำเสียเป็นปัญหาที่รู้จักกันทั่วไป น้ำในแม่น้ำลำคลองในหลาย ๆ ประเทศเต็มไปด้วยสารละลายที่เกิดจากการใช้ปุ๋ยเคมีในการเกษตรกรรม เมื่อน้ำทิ้งไม่มีการกลั่นกรองเมื่อระบายลงสู่แม่น้ำลำคลอง ทำให้น้ำในแม่น้ำลำคลองมีสารเคมีที่เป็นอันตรายเกินกว่าที่มนุษย์จะใช้การได้

เมื่ออุตสาหกรรมเพิ่มมากขึ้น สารที่ทำให้น้ำสกปรกมีมากชนิดขึ้นและมีจำนวนมากขึ้นด้วย แม้จะมีความพยายามที่จะแก้ปัญหานี้ และความก้าวหน้าทางเทคโนโลยีในการที่จะแก้ปัญหาน้ำเสียอันเนื่องจากอุตสาหกรรม แต่ก็ยังมีความกังวลเกี่ยวกับสารเคมีที่ไม่ละลายตัว ซึ่งมีจำนวนที่วัดได้ ทำให้เป็นการยากที่จะแก้ปัญหาน้ำเสียได้อย่างแท้จริง

ผลิตผลของนิเวศน์วิทยาทางทะเล และความสามารถในการขจัดตัวปัญหาที่ทำให้น้ำเสียนั้นขึ้นอยู่กับสัดส่วนทางกายภาพและเคมี ซึ่งมีผลกระทบต่อน้ำจากท่อน้ำทิ้ง และสารเคมีที่ใช้เพื่อการเกษตร น้ำมัน และแร่โลหะ มีการประเมินว่าประมาณ ๒๕ พันล้านตัน ของสิ่งต่าง ๆ ถูกถ่ายทอดลงทะเลโดยผ่านแม่น้ำลำคลองเสียถึงร้อยละ ๙๐

การพัฒนาริมฝั่งชายทะเลมีผลกระทบอย่างยิ่งต่อป่าโกงกาง และแนวหินปะการัง ป่าโกงกางมีความสำคัญยิ่งทางเศรษฐกิจสำหรับประเทศในเขตร้อน ในเวลาล้านปีที่ผ่านมา

ป่าโกงกางเป็นแหล่งที่อยู่สำคัญของพืชและสัตว์ชนิดสำคัญต่าง ๆ นิเวศน์วิทยาของป่าโกงกางสนับสนุนการประมง และเป็นแหล่งที่อยู่สำคัญของปลามากกว่า ๒,๐๐๐ ชนิด รวมทั้งสัตว์เลื้อยคลานและพืช แต่ปรากฏว่าป่าโกงกางที่ได้รับการคุ้มครองจากรัฐบาลมีน้อยกว่าร้อยละ ๑

หินปะการังดูเหมือนจะเป็นระบบนิเวศน์วิทยาที่ได้ผลมากที่สุดในโลก แม้ว่าจะมีเนื้อที่เพียงร้อยละ .๑ ของพื้นผิวโลก ประมาณร้อยละ ๑๐ ของจำนวนปลาที่จับได้ในโลกมีความสัมพันธ์กับปะการัง นอกจากนั้นกลุ่มชนที่อยู่ตามชายทะเลของประเทศในเขตร้อนยังได้พึ่งพาอาศัยปะการังในหลายรูปแบบ แต่ปัจจุบันปะการังกำลังถูกทำลายลงด้วยพิษจากยาฆ่าแมลง

สภาพของดิน

โลกเราในปัจจุบันมีเนื้อที่แผ่นดินที่ใช้ในการเกษตรกรรมประมาณ ๑.๕ พันล้านเฮกแตร์ และประมาณว่าในทุก ๆ ปี เราสูญเสียหน้าดินไป ๒๕ พันล้านตัน ประมาณ ๖ พันล้านเฮกแตร์ หรือร้อยละ ๔๐ ของพื้นผิวโลกเป็นทะเลทราย และทุก ๆ ปีประมาณ ๕–๗ ล้านเฮกแตร์ ของพื้นผิวโลกจะแห้งแล้งเป็นทะเลทราย สาเหตุที่สำคัญคือการที่ปศุสัตว์ทำลายหญ้าและพืชต่างในหน้าแล้ง และการเลี้ยงปศุสัตว์มากเกินไป

สำหรับที่ดินที่มีการชลประทานเข้าถึง ปัญหาของดินแห้งแล้งจนกลายเป็นทะเลทรายมักเนื่องมาจากปัญหาน้ำขัง และน้ำเค็ม ซึ่งส่งผลกระทบทั่วโลก ขณะเดียวกันป่าไม้และป่าละเมาะก็ถูกทำลายเพื่อเผาถ่าน เพื่อการนำไม้ไปใช้ประโยชน์ เพื่อการเกษตรกรรม ฯลฯ การทำลายป่านำไปสู่ปัญหาน้ำท่วม แม่น้ำลำคลองตื้นเขิน และมีผลกระทบต่อพื้นดินที่อยู่ต่ำลงไป

เมื่อถึงปี พ.ศ. ๒๕๔๓ WRI (๒๕๒๙) ได้ศึกษาวิจัยและรายงานว่าจะมีเนื้อที่เพาะปลูกประมาณ .๕ เฮกแตร์ ต่อคน ในโลกที่อุตสาหกรรมเจริญแล้ว และ ๐.๒๕ เฮกแตร์สำหรับแผนเศรษฐกิจปานกลาง และ ๐.๑๙ เฮกแตร์ ในประเทศกำลังพัฒนา นั่นหมายความว่าบริเวณที่มีความต้องการมากกลับมีเนื้อที่พื้นดินที่จะใช้งานได้น้อยลง

ในบรรดาชนิดของดินต่าง ๆ ที่ทำให้ที่ดินกลายเป็นทะเลทรายนั้น ปัญหาเรื่องดินกร่อนเป็นปัญหาที่พบบ่อยกว่าเพื่อน เนื้อดินที่สูญหายไปนี้มักจะถูกพัดพาไปกับลมและน้ำ ปัญหา

ที่ทำให้ควบคุมดินกร่อนได้ยากเพราะบ่อยครั้งสาเหตุที่ทำให้ดินกร่อนนี้อยู่ห่างไกลไปจากที่เกิดเหตุจริง ๆ หลายกิโล ผลกระทบโดยตรงได้แก่การสูญเสียปลาและหินปะการัง สูญเสียพลังน้ำ แหล่งเก็บกักน้ำน้อยลง ในสหรัฐอเมริกา ความสูญเสียของดินกร่อนคิดเป็นมูลค่าถึง ๑๖ พันล้านเหรียญสหรัฐ

จำนวนประชากรที่เพิ่มขึ้นอย่างรวดเร็วเป็นปัญหาโดยตรงต่อระบบการผลิตอาหาร จำนวนประชากรเพิ่มขึ้น แต่เนื้อที่เพื่อการเกษตรกรรมคงเท่าเดิม จึงพบว่ามีความสูญเสียทั้งด้านปริมาณและคุณภาพ เมื่อมีความต้องการอาหารสูงขึ้น การเกษตรกรรมจึงต้องขยายออกไปสู่บริเวณที่เคยใช้เป็นบริเวณกันดินกร่อน ทำให้เทคนิคเดิมในการรักษาดินกร่อนลดน้อยลง

อัตราดินกร่อนแล้วกลายเป็นตะกอนที่พบในแม่น้ำแยงซี คงคา อเมซอน มิสสิสซิปปีและแม่โขง สูงถึง ๓,๘๘๓ พันล้านตันต่อไป

<u>จุดจบของป่าไม้และพืชพรรณ</u>

ป่าในเขตร้อนมีประโยชน์ต่อมนุษย์นานับประการ ทั้งในอุตสาหกรรม การผลิตยา น้ำมัน กาว สี ยาง ฯลฯ รวมไปทั้งการคุ้มครองแหล่งน้ำที่ทำให้ชาวนาที่อยู่ต่ำลงไปมีน้ำใช้โดยสม่ำเสมอ นอกจากนั้นป่าเขตร้อนยังเป็นที่อยู่ที่อาศัยของประชากรกว่า ๒๐๐ ล้านคนที่ได้อาศัยอาหารและแหล่งพำนักพักพิง นอกจากนั้นยังมีสิ่งมีชีวิต พันธุ์ต่าง ๆ มากกว่าป่าในเขตธรรมดา ถึง ๒๐ – ๓๐ เท่า จากรายงานของ WRI (๒๕๒๙) ปรากฏว่า สัตว์ชนิดต่าง ๆ ถึง ๑.๗ ล้านชนิด ที่สามารถระบุได้ โดยทั่วไปเชื่อว่ามี ๕ ล้านชนิด และนักวิทยาศาสตร์หลายคนเชื่อว่ามีกว่า ๑๐ ล้านชนิด และอย่างน้อยร้อยละ ๗๕ เป็นสัตว์ชนิดต่าง ๆ เหล่านี้พบในป่าในเขตร้อน

สัตว์ชนิดต่าง ๆ สูญพันธุ์ไปเป็นเวลานานมาแล้ว แต่อัตราการสูญพันธุ์ทวีขึ้นอย่างรวดเร็วและรุนแรงในสมัยนี้ และบางคนประเมินว่าเมื่อสิ้นศตวรรษนี้สัตว์ต่าง ๆ อาจจะสูญพันธุ์ไปอีกหนึ่งล้านชนิด สาเหตุสำคัญได้แก่การทำลายแหล่งที่อยู่อาศัย โดยเฉพาะป่าเขตร้อน การทำลายป่าเพื่อใช้ไม้เป็นฟืนเพื่อการเกษตรกรรม เพื่อใช้สถานที่เลี้ยงสัตว์ เพื่อก่อสร้างเขื่อน เพื่อบ้านเรือนมนุษย์ และการสร้างทางหลวง ในขณะเดียวกันความพยายามในการ

ปลูกป่าก็เพิ่มมากขึ้น แต่อัตราการทำลายป่าสูงกว่าถึง ๑๐ เท่า นอกจากนั้น การปลูกป่ามักมุ่งเป็นการปลูกพืชชนิดเดียว ซึ่งไม่เหมือนป่าธรรมชาติ และบ่อยครั้งเพื่อการค้า ประมาณการว่าในแต่ละปีจะมีการสูญเสียป่าในเขตร้อนไป ๑๒ ล้านเฮกแตร์

<u>เราจะปรับปรุงสภาพสิ่งแวดล้อมได้อย่างไร?</u>

มาตรการที่ใช้มีมากและต่าง ๆ กัน โดยการทำงานในระดับสถาบันด้วยวิธีการทางเทคนิคและเศรษฐกิจ

ใน พ.ศ.๒๕๑๕ มีประเทศต่าง ๆ ๑๒ ประเทศ ได้จัดตั้งกระทรวงหรือกรมสิ่งแวดล้อมขึ้น และเกือบทุกประเทศมีวิธีการทำนองเดียวกันในการบริหารงานด้านสิ่งแวดล้อม นอกจากนั้นประเทศส่วนมากได้ออกกฎหมายและพระราชกำหนดเพื่อคุ้มครองสิ่งแวดล้อม บางประเทศได้มีการแก้ไขตัวบทกฎหมายให้สอดคล้องกับปัญหาใหม่ ๆ ที่เกิดขึ้น เช่นฝนกรด การทิ้งกากสารเคมีที่เป็นอันตราย

ในระดับภูมิภาค มีการจัดตั้งองค์กรมากขึ้นเพื่อช่วยประสานงานด้านสิ่งแวดล้อมในอาเซียและแปซิฟิครวมทั้งผู้เชี่ยวชาญของกลุ่มอาเซียนในเรื่องสิ่งแวดล้อม โครงการความร่วมมือในอาเซียอาคเณย์เรื่องสิ่งแวดล้อม คณะกรรมการสิ่งแวดล้อมของ OECD มีโครงการที่เข้มแข็งในการเพิ่มพูนความร่วมมือระหว่างสมาชิกในรัฐต่าง ๆ และเมื่อเร็ว ๆ นี้ รัฐมนตรีชาวอัฟริกันทางด้านสิ่งแวดล้อมก็ได้พบปะกันเพื่อเริ่มต้นโครงการไคโร ทางด้านลาตินอเมริกันและแถบทะเลคาริบเบียนก็มีความพยายามทำนองเดียวกัน ความต้องการที่จะให้มีความร่วมมือในระดับภูมิภาคนั้นเห็นได้จากโครงการต่าง ๆ ถึง ๑๑ โครงการของโครงการสิ่งแวดล้อมของสหประชาชาติที่เกี่ยวกับน่านน้ำของภูมิภาค มีผู้เข้าร่วมจาก ๑๒๐ ประเทศ

ในระดับนานาชาติ มีสนธิสัญญาต่าง ๆ มากกว่า ๔๐ ฉบับ ในความพยายามที่จะคุ้มครองสิ่งแวดล้อมและสัตว์ป่า และสนับสนุนการใช้แหล่งทรัพยากรธรรมชาติอย่างมีหลักเกณฑ์และเหตุผล ทั้งนี้ครอบคลุมไปถึงกฎหมายการค้าสากลในการซื้อขายสัตว์ที่กำลังจะสูญพันธ์ และ พ.ศ.๒๕๒๓ ได้มีการวางนโยบายคุ้มครองโลก จัดโดย สหพันธ์นานาชาติแห่งการอนุรักษ์ธรรมชาติและแหล่งทรัพยากรธรรมชาติ (IUCN) ด้วยความร่วมมือและการช่วยเหลือทางการเงินจากโครงการสิ่งแวดล้อมขององค์การสหประชาชาติ (UNEP) และมูลนิธิคุ้มครอง

สัตว์ป่าของโลก (WWF) ด้วยความช่วยเหลือจาก FAO และองค์การ UNESCO

ด้วยความตระหนักในความสำคัญเรื่องการให้การศึกษาในเรื่องสิ่งแวดล้อม โรงเรียนส่วนมากเวลานี้ก็ได้รวมวิชานี้เข้าไว้ในหลักสูตร สื่อการสอนต่าง ๆ ก็ได้มีการพัฒนาและขยายขอบเขตมากขึ้นเพื่อสนับสนุนให้มีการศึกษาในเรื่องสิ่งแวดล้อม นอกจากนี้สถาบันต่าง ๆ ก็เปิดให้มีการสอนหลักสูตรเรื่องสิ่งแวดล้อมมากขึ้น ในอาเซียและแปซิฟิกมีสถาบันอย่างน้อย ๒๘๘ แห่งที่มีหลักสูตรเกี่ยวข้องกับสิ่งแวดล้อม และนับวันก็จะยิ่งเพิ่มหลักสูตรในระดับสูงกว่าปริญญาตรีมากขึ้น

สื่อสารมวลชนก็มีบทบาทสำคัญยิ่งในการสร้างความตื่นตัวในปัญหาเรื่องสิ่งแวดล้อมมากขึ้น หนังสือพิมพ์แทบทุกฉบับ เสนอบทความเกี่ยวกับอุบัติเหตุทางสิ่งแวดล้อม เช่นเหตุการณ์ที่เกิดขึ้นที่เมืองโภปาล ประเทศอินเดีย เมืองเชอร์โนบิล ในสหภาพโซเวียตเป็นต้น ได้รับการเสนอข่าวอย่างกว้างขวาง

ความตื่นตัวที่เพิ่มมากขึ้นนี้ ทำให้ประชาชนสนใจ และเริ่มรู้สึกรับผิดชอบกับสิ่งแวดล้อมมากขึ้น การพัฒนาที่สำคัญที่สุดในช่วงสองทศวรรษที่ผ่านมาคือความรับผิดชอบของมวลชนในการปกป้องธรรมชาติ ทั้งเอกชนและกลุ่มชนได้รวมกันจัดตั้งสมาคมขึ้นเพื่อร่วมกันทำงานอันเป็นปฏิภาคมากขึ้น รวมทั้งขบวนการชิปโกที่พยายามหยุดยั้งการทำลายป่า และขบวนการรักษาป่าของประชาชนในอินเดีย ที่ได้รับความร่วมมือจากชาวบ้านร่วมกันปลูกต้นไม้ ๑ ล้านต้น และโครงการปลูกต้นไม้ ๑๐๐ ล้านต้นในศรีลังกา

มาตรการทางเทคนิคที่จะช่วยแก้ปัญหาก๊าซพิษ ของเหลวและขยะมีหลายวิธี ในประเทศที่มีความเจริญทางอุตสาหกรรมมีการพัฒนาอย่างยิ่งในการขจัดสิ่งปฏิกูลด้วยเทคนิคสมัยใหม่ เช่นในสหรัฐอเมริกา ได้ใช้งบประมาณสูงถึง ๘๖ พันล้านเหรียญอเมริกันในการขจัดของเสีย ใน พ.ศ.๒๕๒๒ นับว่ามากกว่าร้อยละ ๒ ของ GNP งบประมาณจำนวนนี้คาดว่าจะสูงถึง ๑๖๑ พันล้านเหรียญใน พ.ศ.๒๕๓๑ ในญี่ปุ่นได้ใช้งบประมาณในการสร้างมาตรการควบคุมมลพิษ เพิ่มสูงขึ้นจาก ๑๒ พันล้านเหรียญ ใน พ.ศ.๒๕๑๓ เป็น ๖๑ พันล้านเหรียญ ใน พ.ศ.๒๕๑๘

เร็ว ๆ นี้ ได้มีการนำเทคนิคในการทำอุตสาหกรรมโดยไม่ให้มีกากหรือของทิ้งเสียมากขึ้น เพิ่มความระมัดระวังในการใช้วัตถุดิบมากขึ้นและใช้พลังงานอย่างประหยัดขึ้น และกากของเสียน้อยที่สุด

<u>ความต้องการสำหรับอนาคต</u>

เมื่อจำนวนประชากรเพิ่มมากขึ้น ก็ย่อมมีประชากรมากขึ้นที่ปรารถนามาตรฐานความเป็นอยู่ที่ดีและมีคุณภาพ ความต้องการแหล่งทรัพยากรธรรมชาติ ความสุขสำราญทางสิ่งแวดล้อมย่อมเพิ่มมากขึ้นเป็นเงาตามตัว เช่นเดียวกับคุณภาพของสิ่งแวดล้อม ถ้าหากไม่มีการวางนโยบายและแสวงหามาตรการควบคุมการที่จะตอบสนองความต้องการดังกล่าวจะเป็นงานที่ท้าทายยิ่ง สิ่งที่สำคัญยิ่งก็คือระบบการคงอยู่ของชีวิตจะต้องไม่ถูกทำลายจนกระทั่งเกินการแก้ไข

ปัจจุบันมีการยอมรับกันมากขึ้นในแนวความคิดเรื่องการพัฒนาเพื่อการอยู่รอดว่าเป็นวิธีหนึ่งที่จะแก้ปัญหาดังกล่าวได้

กระทรวงและกรมสิ่งแวดล้อมที่ได้ตั้งขึ้นแล้วจะต้องได้รับการสนับสนุน ส่วนมากจะเป็นองค์การใหม่ ทั้งในแง่เศรษฐกิจ และปัจจัยบุคคล ประเทศที่มีกิจกรรมในด้านนี้อยู่แล้วควรจะได้ถ่ายทอดให้แก่ประเทศที่เพิ่งเริ่มต้น ประเด็นที่มีความสำคัญอีกประเด็นหนึ่ง คือการจัดตั้งทิศทางของนโยบายเพื่อนำไปสู่ขั้นตอนการวางแผนในโครงการใดโครงการหนึ่งเพื่อให้โครงการต่าง ๆ ที่ทำส่งผลเต็มที่ ควรจะได้พิจารณาทั้งระดับโครงการและระดับการวางแผนเช่นกัน

แผนพัฒนาของแต่ละประเทศขึ้นอยู่กับขีดคั่นความสามารถทางเศรษฐกิจและรายได้เฉลี่ยของประชากร ฐานะของประเทศนั้นวัดกันที่ปริมาณของแหล่งแร่ น้ำมัน ผลิตผลทางด้านอุตสาหกรรมและเกษตรกรรมเพื่อที่จะพัฒนาประเทศให้เกิดความสัมฤทธิผล จึงมีความจำเป็นที่จะต้องในแนวคิดทาง "บัญชีทางสิ่งแวดล้อม" ดังที่ ดร.เอ็ม.เค.ทอลบา ประธานกรรมการบริหารของโครงการสิ่งแวดล้อมขององค์การสหประชาชาติเคยเสนอไว้ ดังนั้นคุณภาพของน้ำ อากาศ ปริมาณผิวดิน และปัจจัยนิเวศน์วิทยาอื่น ๆ ล้วนเป็นสมบัติของชาติทั้งสิ้น

เมื่อได้มีการจัดตั้งสถาบันสิ่งแวดล้อมขึ้นเมื่อ ๑๐ – ๑๕ ปีก่อนในประเทศใหญ่ ๆ นั้น ส่วนมากได้มุ่งให้ความสำคัญที่การควบคุมมลพิษ เพราะมลพิษจากโรงงานอุตสาหกรรม การคมนาคม และครัวเรือน เป็นเหตุที่ทำลายสิ่งแวดล้อมที่เห็นได้ชัด แต่ปัจจุบันนี้ มีการยอมรับกันมากขึ้นว่า การควบคุมดังกล่าวยังไม่เพียงพอ ยังจะต้องมีมาตรการป้องกันในเรื่องการใช้แหล่งทรัพยากร และผลกระทบที่มีต่อสิ่งแวดล้อมในขั้นที่สองและที่สาม โดยเฉพาะส่วนที่มีผลกระทบต่อสภาพสังคมและวัฒนธรรม นอกจากนี้องค์กรที่ได้รับการอบรมในเรื่องการควบคุมมลพิษ ควรจะได้รับการศึกษาในวงกว้างถึงการบริหารสิ่งแวดล้อมด้วย มิฉะนั้น เขาจะไม่สามารถมองเห็นภาพรวม ในการวางแผน และนำความเข้าใจในเรื่องสิ่งแวดล้อมไปสู่ภาคปฏิบัติเพื่อการพัฒนาเพื่อความอยู่รอดได้

ในขณะที่ประเทศต่าง ๆ ได้มีการออกกฎหมายคุ้มครองสิ่งแวดล้อม แต่ก็ยังไม่ค่อยมีผลในด้านปฏิบัติ ด้วยขาดปัจจัยทางด้านบุคลากร การเงิน และข้อมูลในการแก้ปัญหาที่มีประสิทธิภาพที่สุด ข้อจำกัดต่าง ๆ เหล่านี้ เห็นได้ชัดในประเทศกำลังพัฒนา การที่จะทำให้กฎหมายมีผลใช้บังคับ จึงจำเป็นต้องมีการชักจูงใจ และมีการช่วยสนับสนุนในการบริหารงานสิ่งแวดล้อม

ในช่วงสองทศวรรษที่ผ่านมา มวลชนมีความรู้มากขึ้นเกี่ยวกับการสูญเสียของโลก มวลชนจะต้องได้รับข้อมูลต่าง ๆ เพิ่มมากขึ้น ทั้งนี้ควรจะหมายรวมทั้งสายงานต่าง ๆ ที่เกี่ยวกับกิจกรรมที่พยายามส่งเสริมสภาพแวดล้อม จะต้องชี้ให้เห็นว่ามีวิธีแก้ไขเพื่อมิให้มวลชนเกิดความรู้สึกหมดหวังและท้อถอย

เป็นที่ยอมรับกันโดยทั่วไปว่า กิจกรรมใดก็ตามที่จะให้ผลเต็มที่จะต้องเริ่มมาจากรากฐานของสังคมนั้น ๆ ประชาชนจะต้องมีส่วนร่วมในวิธีการที่ยอมรับบทบาทของปัจเจกบุคคล

หน้าที่และการกระทำของบุคคลย่อมมีอิทธิพลยิ่ง ต่อคุณภาพของสิ่งแวดล้อม และแหล่งทรัพยากรธรรมชาติ ที่มีต่อบุคคลอื่น ดังนั้นหน้าที่และการกระทำของประชาชนแต่ละคนเมื่อรวมกันแล้วก็จะมีอิทธิพลสำคัญยิ่ง ดังนั้นจึงจำเป็นที่จะต้องสร้างความสนใจ ความร่วมมือในระดับประชาชน ในการให้ความสำคัญแก่คุณค่าทางจริยธรรม ความเมตตา กรุณา ความอดทน

ที่พึงมีต่อสรรพชีวิตทั้งปวง ความเคารพที่พึงมีต่อชีวิตทุกรูปแบบ ความบรรสานใน ธรรมชาติ มากกว่าความรู้สึกหยิ่งยะโสปรารถนาที่จะเป็นจ้าวธรรมชาติ รับผิดชอบในการถนอมธรรมชาติ เพื่อประโยชน์สุขในปัจจุบัน และสำหรับอนุชนในอนาคต สิ่งเหล่านี้เป็นท่าทีและการปฏิบัติขั้นพื้นฐานที่จะต้องสนับสนุนและพัฒนาให้มั่นคงขึ้น

สมเด็จพระสัมมาสัมพุทธเจ้าทรงเห็นความสำคัญในหลักจริยธรรมเหล่านี้ ทรงสอนและทรงปฏิบัติเป็นแบบอย่างนานกว่า ๒,๐๐๐ ปีมาแล้ว หลักจริยธรรมเหล่านี้ยังใช้ได้ดีในสังคมปัจจุบัน ความต้องการสำหรับปัจจุบันและอนาคต คือการให้แต่ละคนมีความตระหนักในพื้นฐานที่สำคัญของจริยธรรมที่เกี่ยวกับสิ่งแวดล้อม และนำไปสู่ภาคปฏิบัติ

ดร. เน ทุน เป็นชาวพุทธ เป็นประธานภาคพื้นและผู้แทนของอาเซียและปาซิฟิก ในโครงการสิ่งแวดล้อมขององค์การสหประชาชาติ (UNEP) ได้เข้ามาทำงานตำแหน่งนี้ ตั้งแต่ พ.ศ. ๒๕๐๙ เคยเป็นศาสตราจารย์ วิศวกรรมสิ่งแวดล้อมที่สถาบันเทคโนโลยีแห่งอาเซีย และเคยทำงานให้กับบริษัทพลังงานนานาชาติ บทความชิ้นนี้เขียนขึ้นเป็นงานส่วนตัว

โครงการพระพุทธศาสนาเพื่อธรรมชาติ

แนนซี่ แนช

"โลกเล็กลงทุกที และต้องพึ่งพาอาศัยกันมากขึ้น ....ทุกวันนี้ ยิ่งกว่าที่แล้วมา จะต้องอธิบายชีวิตในความหมายที่มีความรับผิดชอบต่อจักรวาลมากขึ้น มิใช่แต่เพียงความรับผิดชอบระหว่างชาติต่อชาติ มนุษย์ต่อมนุษย์เท่านั้น แต่มนุษย์ยังต้องรับผิดชอบชีวิตในรูปแบบอื่นๆ ด้วย"

พระพุทธศาสนาเพื่อธรรมชาติเป็นโครงการที่ก่อตั้งขึ้นเพื่อเสริมสร้างความตระหนักและการกระทำอันมีความห่วงใยต่อสิ่งแวดล้อมทางธรรมชาติ โดยมีรากฐานมาจากพระราชดำรัสขององค์ดาไลลามะ ดังปรากฏข้างต้น ในการประทานสัมภาษณ์ เมื่อ พ.ศ.2522 และโครงการนี้ได้กำลังใจและการสนับสนุนจากพระองค์ท่านผู้ทรงเป็นผู้นำชาวพุทธของโลก

งานของเรามีทั้งงานวิจัย ค้นคว้า รวบรวม เพื่อผลิตสื่อการสอนในเชิงพุทธศาสนา เพื่อให้มนุษย์มีความรับผิดชอบต่อโลกและชีวิตทั้งปวง บทเรียนและงานศิลปที่ได้จากวรรณกรรมพุทธศาสนามีความเก่าแก่นานกว่า 2500 ปี แม้กระนั้นก็ยังใช้ได้ผลสำหรับทุกวันนี้ เช่นเดียวกับในสมัยก่อน และสามารถสื่อกับสังคมปัจจุบันได้ในหลายรูปแบบ

การที่เลือกพระพุทธศาสนาให้เป็นโครงการริเริ่มในแนวใหม่ คือ การให้การศึกษาทางด้านสิ่งแวดล้อมนั้น เพราะพระพุทธศาสนาเป็นศาสนาที่มีมาแต่ดั้งเดิม มีปรัชญาและมีคำสอนที่เน้นให้มีความตระหนักและมีความเมตตาต่อชีวิตทั้งมวล

ศรัทธาเป็นปัจจัยที่มีอิทธิพลสำคัญในภูมิภาคอาเซีย ซึ่งเป็นบริเวณที่ชีวิตสัตว์พืชพรรณ และแหล่งที่อยู่อาศัย กำลังถูกทำลายลงอย่างรวดเร็ว และได้ปรากฏแล้วว่า ศรัทธาเป็นปัจจัยสำคัญที่มีอิทธิพลโดยตรงต่อการคุ้มครองชีวิตสัตว์และแหล่งที่อยู่อาศัย

เท่าที่เป็นมา การอนุรักษ์ยังมีผลเพียงการคุ้มครองแบบไม่รุกราน ตัวอย่างเช่น แหล่งที่อยู่อาศัยของสัตว์ในบริเวณวัด นับว่าเป็นเขตคุ้มครองสำหรับชาวพุทธ

ในประเทศไทย วินัยของพระที่อยู่ป่ายังคงรักษาอย่างเคร่งครัด บริเวณวัดจึงได้รับการคุ้มครองโดยธรรมชาติ ในประเทศธิเบต ก็เป็นเช่นนั้น จนกระทั่งเมื่อจีนเข้ายึดครองใน พ.ศ.2493 ธิเบตเคยเป็นประเทศที่ประชาชนและสัตว์ป่าอยู่ด้วยกันด้วยความบรรสานยิ่ง

อย่างไรก็ตาม วิกฤติการณ์ทางสิ่งแวดล้อมที่เราเผชิญอยู่ทุกวันนี้ ต้องการความช่วยเหลือที่เข้มแข็ง และชาวพุทธทั่วโลกซึ่งมีประมาณ 500 ล้านคนนั้น น่าจะมีอิทธิพลเพียงพอถ้าเป็นนักอนุรักษ์ที่เข้มแข็ง

การมุ่งเน้นคุณค่าทางด้านจิตวิญญาณของมนุษย์และวัฒนธรรม มิได้หมายความว่าจะละเลยบทบาทของวิทยาศาสตร์ ซึ่งที่จริงแล้วก็เป็นส่วนหนึ่งของวัฒนธรรมของมนุษย์ด้วย โครงการของเราตระหนักดีว่า วิทยาศาสตร์มีบทบาทสำคัญ แต่ก่อนอื่นเราจะต้องหันเหความสนใจของนักการศึกษาและผู้มีอำนาจในการตัดสินใจ และจากนั้น นักวิทยา-ศาสตร์ก็จะสามารถช่วยแก้ภัยพิบัติของสิ่งแวดล้อมซึ่งเรากำลังเผชิญหน้า อันเป็นผลมาจากความโง่เขลา ความโลภ และการขาดความเคารพต่อโลก

นักวิทยาศาสตร์จะชี้ให้เห็นและพิสูจน์ว่า ประสิทธิภาพของโลกในการรองรับชีวิตนั้น กำลังถดถอยลงไปในช่วงที่มีความต้องการสูง....ในขณะที่จำนวนประชากรเพิ่มมากขึ้น ความคาดหวังสูงขึ้น และพลังการใช้ก็เพิ่มทวีขึ้น

แต่วิทยาศาสตร์มีขอบเขตอยู่กับสภาพของโลก ในขณะที่ศาสนาและวัฒนธรรมประเพณีเป็นแหล่งคุณค่าของมนุษย์ และทุกวันนี้ ประชาชนจำนวนมากรู้สึกว่า นอกเสียจากปัจเจกชนและค่านิยมทางสังคมจะได้รับการกระตุ้น เมื่อนั้นเราจึงจะเริ่มแก้ปัญหาที่กำลังเผชิญอยู่ได้ในวิถีทางที่จะมีผลต่อชีวิตบนโลก ทั้งในปัจจุบัน และอนาคต

สำหรับโครงการเช่นนี้ ความสำคัญของงานทางวิชาการเป็นสิ่งที่ไม่อาจมองข้ามไปได้ และเราก็โชคดี นับแต่เริ่มโครงการ เรามีนักวิชาการที่มีคุณภาพจากสถาบันที่ทรงเกียรติเข้ามาทำงานให้กับโครงการ

สภาเพื่อการศาสนาและวัฒนธรรม และสำนักข่าวขององค์ดาไลลามะได้ให้คำแนะนำในการศึกษาฝ่ายมหายาน ในทางเถรวาท มูลนิธิคุ้มครองสัตว์ป่าฯแห่งประเทศไทยเป็นผู้รับผิดชอบ โดยมีนักวิชาการจากกระทรวงศึกษาธิการและมหาวิทยาลัยธรรม

ศาสตร์ หัวหน้านักวิชาการของเรา...ดร ฉัตรสุมาลย์ กบิลสิงห์ ที่กรุงเทพ และพระภิกษุกรรมะเก๋เล็กยูท้อก ที่เมืองธารัมศาลา ประเทศอินเดีย พร้อมนักวิชาการร่วมทีมได้ช่วยกันทำงานวิจัย เขียนและแปล ได้ทำงานเป็นที่น่าพอใจในการศึกษาวรรณกรรมและประวัติศาสตร์อย่างกว้างขวางในระยะเวลาจำกัด

นายโลดี กยารี รัฐมนตรีช่วยว่าการกระทรวงศึกษาธิการ ในองค์ดาไลลามะ เป็นผู้ประสานงานฝ่ายธิเบต และผู้ประสานงานฝ่ายไทย ได้แก่ อาจารย์ศิระจิต วรมนตรี กรรมการมูลนิธิคุ้มครองสัตว์ป่าฯแห่งประเทศไทย ทั้งสองท่านได้สละเวลา แรงกายและความสร้างสรรในการทำงานจนทำให้หนังสือนี้เป็นรูปเล่มขึ้นมา นับเป็นงานชิ้นแรกในผลิตผลเพื่อการศึกษาหลายรูปแบบที่โครงการได้ดำริไว้

ชาวพุทธทั้งธิเบตและไทย ได้ริเริ่มงานนี้ขึ้นเป็นครั้งแรก ด้วยเหตุผลง่ายๆที่ว่าพวกเขามีความเห็นใจและเป็นบุคคลที่ยินยอมที่จะรับภาระงาน การติดต่อกับชาวพุทธในสังคมและประเทศอื่นๆ ย่อมติดตามมาในโอกาสต่อไป และโครงการมีความยินดีต้อนรับทุกๆท่าน

เนื่องจากทั่วโลกกำลังมีความตื่นตัวในการอนุรักษ์ โครงการนี้นับแต่แรกเริ่มจึงได้มองเห็นว่า แม้จะมีความสำคัญสำหรับกลุ่มชาวพุทธเป็นกลุ่มแรก แต่ก็สามารถถือเป็นต้นแบบในงานวิจัยสำหรับโครงการประเภทเดียวกัน ที่อาจจะทำได้ในศาสนาและวัฒนธรรมอื่นๆด้วย

พระพุทธศาสนาเพื่อการอนุรักษ์มีเป้าหมายในการทำโครงการตัวอย่าง เพื่อผลิตสื่อและวัสดุการสอน สำหรับชนต่างกลุ่ม ทั้งระดับรัฐบาล เอกชน กลุ่มชาวพุทธ และกลุ่มศาสนิกอื่นที่อาจสนใจศึกษาและนำไปใช้ ทุกคนที่มีส่วนร่วมในโครงการนี้ มีความประทับใจ และได้รับแรงบันดาลใจจากการที่เอกชนและหน่วยงานทั้งหลายให้ความสนใจจากส่วนต่างๆของโลก จากศาสนาและวัฒนธรรมต่างๆกัน ที่เห็นว่า โครงการนี้มิได้เป็นเพียงการตอบรับปัญหาด้านนิเวศน์วิทยาเท่านั้น แต่ยังเป็นปัจจัยในการฟื้นฟูจริยธรรมในทางสิ่งแวดล้อมซึ่งกำลังเป็นที่ต้องการอย่างสูง